Bloom's

GUIDES

Zora Neale Hurston's
Their Eyes Were Watching God

The Adventures of Huckleberry Finn

All the Pretty Horses

Animal Farm

The Autobiography of Malcolm X

The Awakening

The Bell Jar

Beloved

Beowulf

Black Boy

The Bluest Eye

Brave New World

The Canterbury Tales

Catch-22

The Catcher in the Rye

The Chosen

The Crucible

Cry, the Beloved Country

Death of a Salesman

Fahrenheit 451

A Farewell to Arms

Frankenstein

The Glass Menagerie

The Grapes of Wrath

Great Expectations

The Great Gatsby

Hamlet

The Handmaid's Tale

Heart of Darkness

The House on Mango Street

I Know Why the Caged Bird Sings

The Iliad

Invisible Man

Jane Eyre

The Joy Luck Club

The Kite Runner

Lord of the Flies

Macbeth

Maggie: A Girl of the Streets

The Member of the Wedding

The Metamorphosis

Native Son

Night

1984

The Odyssey

Oedipus Rex

Of Mice and Men

One Hundred Years of Solitude

Pride and Prejudice

Ragtime

A Raisin in the Sun

The Red Badge of Courage

Romeo and Juliet

The Scarlet Letter

A Separate Peace

Slaughterhouse-Five

Snow Falling on Cedars

The Stranger

A Streetcar Named Desire

The Sun Also Rises

A Tale of Two Cities

Their Eyes Were Watching God

The Things They Carried

To Kill a Mockingbird

Uncle Tom's Cabin

The Waste Land

Wuthering Heights

Bloom's
GUIDES

Zora Neale Hurston's
Their Eyes Were Watching God

Edited & with an Introduction
by Harold Bloom

BLOOM'S
LITERARY CRITICISM
An imprint of Infobase Publishing

Bloom's Guides: Their Eyes Were Watching God

Copyright © 2009 by Infobase Publishing

Introduction © 2009 by Harold Bloom

All rights reserved. No part of this book may be reproduced or utilized in any form or by any means, electronic or mechanical, including photocopying, recording, or by any information storage or retrieval systems, without permission in writing from the publisher. For information contact:

Bloom's Literary Criticism
An imprint of Infobase Publishing
132 West 31st Street
New York, NY 10001

Library of Congress Cataloging-in-Publication Data
Zora Neale Hurston's Their eyes were watching God / edited and with an introduction by Harold Bloom.
    p. cm. — (Bloom's guides)
Includes bibliographical references and index.
ISBN 978-1-60413-571-8
    1. Hurston, Zora Neale. Their eyes were watching God. 2. African American women in literature. 3. African Americans in literature.
    I. Bloom, Harold. II. Title. III. Series.
PS3515.U789T639 2009
813'.52—dc22

                                    2009015016

Bloom's Literary Criticism books are available at special discounts when purchased in bulk quantities for businesses, associations, institutions, or sales promotions. Please call our Special Sales Department in New York at (212) 967–8800 or (800) 322–8755.

You can find Bloom's Literary Criticism on the World Wide Web at
http://www.chelseahouse.com

Contributing Editor: Portia Weiskel
Cover design by Takeshi Takahashi
Printed in the United States of America
IBT IBT 10 9 8 7 6 5 4 3 2 1
This book is printed on acid-free paper.

All links and Web addresses were checked and verified to be correct at the time of publication. Because of the dynamic nature of the Web, some addresses and links may have changed since publication and may no longer be valid.

Contents

Introduction

I

Extraliterary factors have entered into the process of even secular canonization from Hellenistic Alexandria into the High Modernist Era of Eliot and Pound, so that it need not much dismay us if contemporary work by women and by minority writers becomes esteemed on grounds other than aesthetic. When the High Modernist critic Hugh Kenner assures us of the permanent eminence of the novelist and polemicist Wyndham Lewis, we can be persuaded, unless of course we actually read books like *Tarr* and *Hitler.* Reading Lewis is a rather painful experience and makes me skeptical of Kenner's canonical assertions. In the matter of Zora Neale Hurston, I have had a contrary experience, starting with skepticism when I first encountered essays by her admirers, let alone by her idolators. Reading *Their Eyes Were Watching God* dispels all skepticism. *Moses: Man of the Mountain* is an impressive book in its mode and ambitions but a mixed achievement, unable to resolve problems of diction and of rhetorical stance. Essentially, Hurston is the author of one superb and moving novel, unique not in its kind but in its isolated excellence among other stories of the kind.

The wistful opening of *Their Eyes Were Watching God* pragmatically affirms greater repression in women as opposed to men, by which I mean "repression" only in Freud's sense, unconscious yet purposeful forgetting:

> Now, women forget all those things they don't want to remember, and remember everything they don't want to forget. The dream is the truth. Then they act and do things accordingly.

7

Hurston's Janie is now necessarily a paradigm for women, of whatever race, heroically attempting to assert their own individuality in contexts that continue to resent and fear any consciousness that is not male. In a larger perspective, should the contexts modify, the representation of Janie will take its significant place in a long tradition of such representations in American and English fiction. This tradition extends from Samuel Richardson to Doris Lessing and other contemporaries, but only rarely has it been able to visualize authentically strong women who begin with all the deprivations that circumstance assigns to Janie. It is a crucial aspect of Hurston's subtle sense of limits that the largest limitation is that imposed upon Janie by her grandmother, who loves her best, yet fears for her the most.

As a former slave, the grandmother, Nanny, is haunted by the compensatory dream of making first her daughter, and then her granddaughter, something other than "the mule of the world," customary fate of the black woman. The dream is both powerful enough, and sufficiently unitary, to have driven Janie's mother away and to condemn Janie herself to a double disaster of marriages, before the tragic happiness of her third match completes as much of her story as Hurston desires to give us. As readers, we carry away with us what Janie never loses, the vivid pathos of her grandmother's superb and desperate displacement of hope:

> "And, Janie, maybe it wasn't much, but Ah done de best Ah kin by you. Ah raked and scraped and bought dis lil piece uh land so you wouldn't have to stay in de white folks' yard and tuck yo' head befo' other chillum at school. Dat was all right when you was little. But when you got big enough to understand things, Ah wanted you to look upon yo'self. Ah don't want yo' feathers always crumpled by folks throwin' up things in yo' face. And Ah can't die easy thinkin' maybe de menfolks white or black is makin' a spit cup outa you: Have some sympathy fuh me. Put me down easy, Janie, Ah'm a cracked plate."

II

Hurston's rhetorical strength, even in *Their Eyes Were Watching God*, is frequently too overt, and threatens an excess, when contrasted with the painful simplicity of her narrative line and the reductive tendency at work in all her characters except for Janie and Nanny. Yet the excess works, partly because Hurston is so considerable and knowing a mythologist. Hovering in *Their Eyes Were Watching God* is the Mosaic myth of deliverance, the pattern of revolution and exodus that Hurston reimagines as her prime trope of power:

> But there are other concepts of Moses abroad in the world. Asia and all the Near East are sown with legends of this character. They are so numerous and so varied that some students have come to doubt if the Moses of the Christian concept is real. Then Africa has her mouth on Moses. All across the continent there are the legends of the greatness of Moses, but not because of his beard nor because he brought the laws down from Sinai. No, he is revered because he had the power to go up the mountain and to bring them down. Many men could climb mountains. Anyone could bring down laws that had been handed to them. But who can talk with God face to face? Who has the power to command God to go to a peak of a mountain and there demand of Him laws with which to govern a nation? What other man has ever commanded the wind and the hail? The light and darkness? That calls for power, and that is what Africa sees in Moses to worship. For he is worshipped as a god.

Power in Hurston is always *potentia*, the demand for life, for more life. Despite the differences in temperament, Hurston has affinitied both with Dreiser and with Lawrence, heroic vitalists. Her art, like theirs, exalts an exuberance that is beauty, a difficult beauty because it participates in reality-testing. What is strongest in Janie is a persistence akin to Dreiser's

Carrie and Lawrence's Ursula and Gudrun, a drive to survive in one's own fashion. Nietzsche's vitalistic injunction, that we must try to live as though it were morning, is the implicit basis of Hurston's true religion, which in its American formulation (Thoreau's) reminds us that only that day dawns to which we are alive. Something of Lawrence's incessant sense of the sun is paralleled by Hurston's trope of solar trajectory, in a cosmos where: "They sat on the boarding house porch and saw the sun plunge into the same crack in the earth from which the night emerged" and where: "Every morning the world flung itself over and exposed the town to the sun."

Janie's perpetual sense of the possibilities of another day propels her from Nanny's vision of safety first to the catastrophe of Joe Starks and then to the love of Tea Cake, her true husband. But to live in a way that starts with the sun is to become pragmatically doom-eager, since mere life is deprecated in contrast to the possibility of glory, or life more abundant, rather than Nanny's dream of a refuge from exploitation. Hurston's most effective irony is that Janie's drive toward her own erotic potential should transcend her grandmother's categories, since the marriage with Tea Cake is also Janie's pragmatic liberation from bondage to men. When he tells her, in all truth, that she has the keys to the kingdom, he frees her from living in her grandmother's way.

A more pungent irony drove Hurston to end Janie's idyll with Tea Cake's illness and the ferocity of his subsequent madness. The impulse of her own vitalism compels Janie to kill him in self-defense, thus ending necessarily life and love in the name of the possibility of more life again. The novel's conclusion is at once an elegy and a vision of achieved peace, an intense realization that indeed we are all asleep in the outer life:

> The day of the gun, and the bloody body, and the courthouse came and commenced to sing a sobbing sigh out of every corner in the room; out of each and every chair and thing. Commenced to sing, commenced to sob and sigh, singing and sobbing. Then Tea Cake came prancing around her where she was and the song of the

sigh flew out of the window and lit in the top of the pine trees. Tea Cake, with the sun for a shawl. Of course he wasn't dead. He could never be dead until she herself had finished feeling and thinking. The kiss of his memory made pictures of love and light against the wall. Here was peace. She pulled in her horizon like a great fish-net. Pulled it from around the waist of the world and draped it over her shoulder. So much of life in its meshes! She called in her soul to come and see.

III

Hurston herself was refreshingly free of all the ideologies that currently obscure the reception of her best book. Her sense of power has nothing in common with politics of any persuasion, with contemporary modes of feminism, or even with those questers who search for a black aesthetic. As a vitalist, she was of the line of the Wife of Bath and Sir John Falstaff and Mynheer Peeperkorn. Like them, she was outrageous, heroically larger than life, witty in herself and the cause of wit in others. She belongs now to literary legend, which is as it should be. Her famous remark in response to Carl Van Vechten's photographs is truly the epigraph to her life and work: "I love myself when I am laughing. And then again when I am looking mean and impressive." Walt Whitman would have delighted in that as in her assertion: "When I set my hat at a certain angle and saunter down Seventh Avenue . . . the cosmic Zora emerges. . . . How *can* any deny themselves the pleasure of my company? It's beyond me." With Whitman, Hurston herself is now an image of American literary vitality and a part also of the American mythology of exodus, of the power to choose the party of Eros, of more life.

Biographical Sketch

Zora Neale Hurston was born probably on January 7, 1891, although she frequently gave her birth date as 1901 or 1903. She was born and raised in America's first all-black incorporated town, Eatonville, Florida. Her father, John Hurston, was a former sharecropper who became a carpenter, preacher, and three-term mayor of Eatonville. Her mother, Lucy Hurston, died in 1904; two weeks after her death, Hurston was sent to Jacksonville, Florida, to attend school, but wound up neglected by her remarried father and worked a variety of menial jobs. A five-year gap in her personal history at this time has led some biographers to conjecture that she was married; however, no evidence exists to support or disprove this speculation. In 1917 she began studies at Morgan Academy in Baltimore and in 1918 attended Howard University, where her first short story appeared in the college literary magazine. She later won a scholarship to Barnard College to study with the eminent anthropologist Franz Boas.

While living in New York, Hurston worked as a secretary to the popular novelist Fannie Hurst. Though she only lived in New York for a short time, Hurston is considered a major force in the Harlem Renaissance of the 1920s and 1930s. She was an associate editor for the one-issue avant-garde journal *Fire!!* and she collaborated on several plays with various writers, including *Mule Bone: A Comedy of Negro Life*, written with Langston Hughes. Boas arranged a fellowship for Hurston that allowed her to travel throughout the South and collect folklore. The result of these travels was the publication of Hurston's first collection of black folktales, *Mules and Men* (1935). Hurston is thought to be the first black American to have collected and published Afro-American folklore, and both of her collections have become much-used sources for myths and legends of black culture. Her interest in anthropology took her to several Latin American countries, including Jamaica, Haiti, and Honduras. Her experiences in Jamaica and Haiti appear in her second collection of folktales, *Tell My Horse* (1938).

Hurston's first novel, *Jonah's Gourd Vine* (1934), is loosely based on the lives of her parents in Eatonville. It was written shortly after *Mules and Men* (although it was published first) and has been criticized as being more of an anthropological study than a novel. Her best-known work, the novel *Their Eyes Were Watching God*, was published in 1937. Written after a failed love affair, *Their Eyes Were Watching God* focuses on a middle-aged woman's quest for fulfillment in an oppressive society. Hurston also wrote *Moses, Man of the Mountain* (1939), an attempt to fuse biblical narrative and folk myth. In addition to her life as a writer, Hurston worked temporarily as a teacher, a librarian at an air force base, a staff writer at Paramount Studios, and a reporter for the *Fort Pierce [Florida] Chronicle*.

Her autobiography, *Dust Tracks on a Road*, won the 1943 Annisfield Award. Her final novel, *Seraph on the Suwanee*, appeared in 1948. An attempt to universalize the issues addressed in *Their Eyes Were Watching God, Seraph* is Hurston's only novel to feature white protagonists. Hurston's other honors include Guggenheim Fellowships in 1936 and 1938. She wrote for various magazines in the 1950s, but her increasingly conservative views concerning race relations effectively alienated her from black intellectual culture. She died on January 28, 1960, in Fort Pierce, Florida.

The Story Behind the Story

"Colored People of the United States: Solve the great race problem by securing a home in Eatonville, Florida, a Negro city governed by negroes" (*Understanding Zora Neale Hurston's "Their Eyes Were Watching God"* 148). This announcement from *The Eatonville Speaker* in 1889 is one of several examples of actual events or places that form the structure—and contribute to the vibrancy—of *Their Eyes Were Watching God*. Another is the porch of Joe Clark's general store in Eatonville—and all the front porches in town—where the people sit in their rocking chairs to pass the time, expedite the perennial flow of gossip, "pass nations through their mouths . . . [and sit] in judgment" (3).

The hurricane that kills uncountable numbers of migrant workers and that Janie and Tea Cake barely survive, was, according to Massachusetts Institute of Technology atmospheric scientist Kerry Emanuel, also a real event. In 1928 a hurricane ravaged both coastal and inland areas of Florida, bringing torrential rains that broke the dikes of Lake Okeechobee. And, as the novel relates, no warning system was in place or helping services for search and rescue. Huddled against the frail walls of their makeshift shelters, Janie and Tea Cake and their friends looking up at the tempest in the skies must have thought they were seeing Death itself, thus, perhaps, the title, *Their Eyes Were Watching God*.

Two real experiences in Hurston's personal life also influenced her story, one she explicitly acknowledged. Janie, her memorable protagonist, has three encounters with death in the novel, two of them face to face and particularly unnerving. According to Hurston biographer Robert Hemenway, the death of her mother was made more traumatic than it might have been, when Hurston, only nine years old, was involuntarily pulled into a struggle for dominance over her mother's deathbed requests that were summarily thwarted by the community of mourners intent on keeping the old customs. Hemenway relates that Hurston "agonized" for years over this memory, and she herself wrote in her autobiography, "If there is any consciousness after death, I hope that Mama knows that I did my best [to carry out her wishes]. She must know how I have suffered for my failure" (*Dust Tracks on a Road* 176).

The most dramatic influence is the resemblance between Janie's love affair with Tea Cake and Hurston's own with a man she evasively identifies in her autobiography as "P. M. P." Scholars have since discovered his identity, but the point is the passionate and tenacious quality of both relationships. Hurston describes falling in love with her mystery man as "a parachute jump" (*Dust Tracks* 205). Like Janie, Hurston was significantly older than her lover, and, like Tea Cake, "P. M. P." was acknowledged by Hurston to be sexually dominant and sometimes violent. Hurston wrote *Their Eyes* in the three weeks following the tumultuous denouement of this relationship. Reflecting later on this extremely painful episode, she confesses that in her writing she had "tried to embalm all the tenderness of [her] passion for him" (*Dust Tracks* 188–189). In her analysis of the novel, Diana Miles writes, "Her use of the word 'embalm' is a telling choice for describing the end of a violent relationship; the relevance of her word choice becomes apparent in the fictional scene where Janie and Tea Cake's affair ends because she shoots him as he is about to attack her. . . . Ultimately, *Their Eyes* reflects Hurston's own vulnerability to male domination" (*Women, Violence and Testimony in the Works of Zora Neale Hurston* 51).

When *Their Eyes* first appeared in 1937, it was memorably greeted by these disparaging words from Richard Wright:

> Miss Hurston seems to have no desire whatsoever to move in the direction of serious fiction. . . . [She] can write; but her prose is cloaked in that facile sensuality that has dogged Negro expression since the days of Phyllis Wheatley. . . . Her characters eat and laugh and cry and work and kill; they swing like a pendulum eternally in that safe and narrow orbit in which America likes to see the Negro live: between laughter and tears. (*New Masses*, October 5, 1935; reprinted in *Critical Essays* 75).

Another reviewer was less dismissive but noted more limitations than talent in the novel: "It isn't that this novel is bad, but it deserves to be better" (Otis Ferguson, *New Republic*, October 13, 1937; reprinted in *Critical Essays* 77). There was some praise.

Reviewing the novel for the *New York Herald Tribune Books* (September 26, 1937), Sheila Hibben applauded Hurston for "[writing] with her head as well as with her heart" and for her "warm, vibrant touch" in rendering "a flashing, gleaming riot of black people, with a limitless sense of humor, and a wild, strange sadness" (reprinted in *Critical Essays* 73–74). But mainly, the black writers of the Harlem Renaissance—proudly determined as they were to redefine Negro life with its African origins and to protest against the white violence implicit in Jim Crow era behavior and the condescension of Northern "liberal" attitudes—resisted writers, who, in their view, were looking backward by choosing to depict stereotypical characters in insular settings. The harsh charges leveled against writers like Hurston included accusations of pandering to white readers who didn't want to be disturbed by angry portrayals of overt racism or Negroes with black pride.

Hurston did in fact have patrons (other black writers did as well)—three rich, white, liberal women interested in supporting young black writers—but, interestingly, according to Hurston biographer Robert Hemenway, Hurston published nothing of significance during her patronage period, which ended five years before she wrote and published *Their Eyes*. In the end, the sentiments and powerful motivations generated by the Harlem Renaissance writers prevailed and Hurston's novel dropped out of sight, eventually going out of print. It didn't re-emerge until the decades of the seventies and eighties.

The writer Alice Walker is regarded as being principally instrumental in reintroducing Hurston and her work to the public. Having come upon the novel herself and been much moved and impressed, she set out to find Hurston's unmarked burial site. Finding it after much effort in the Garden of Heavenly Rest, a segregated cemetery in Fort Pierce, Florida, she installed an appropriate and lasting marker that included these words: "A Genius of the South." Just a few years earlier, in 1970–71, Robert Hemenway was awarded a National Endowment for the Humanities grant to do research on Hurston and her work. The result of his labors was the 1977 biography *Zora Neale Hurston: A Literary Biography*. In her foreword to the biography, Alice Walker concluded with these words: "*We are a people. A people do not throw their geniuses away. If they do, it is our duty as witnesses for the future* to collect them again for the sake of our children. If necessary, bone by bone" (*Foreword* xviii).

In 1978 the University of Illinois republished Hurston's novel. Several cultural trends combined to help bring *Their Eyes* into the purview of established literary circles, where its value and status in the canon of established American literature generate often heated debate. The impact of feminist writing, renewed interest specifically in black women writers, and, in general, the energies driving multicultural interests were—and still are—among these influences. One other explanation of Janie Crawford's appeal for diverse groups of readers is that she is engaged in a struggle that is not essentially about being a black or a white person; she is pursuing the more universal goals of love and authenticity.

The novel continues to be discussed in the controversial categories of "reception politics." Among the interesting new issues for discussion is the observation recently made by Todd McGowan in *The Feminine "No!"* (2001) that the quality readers find most appealing about Janie and Tea Cake's relationship—their "playfulness"—is precisely what Richard Wright disparaged as the book's unforgivable "non-political-ness." Another new issue is whether the novel can be read as a "feminist" story raised by critics who assert that Tea Cake is actually not very different in style or attitude from the first two men in Janie's life whom she rejects. But the novel is now widely read and widely acclaimed. A made-for-television film adaptation of the novel starring Halle Berry came out in 2005 and visitors to Eatonville, Florida, can find more than a well-marked grave. An annual Zora Neale Hurston Street Festival of the Arts and Humanities is sponsored each January by the Association to Preserve the Eatonville Community.

List of Characters

Janie Crawford Killicks Starks Woods is the protagonist of the novel. Her long, beautiful hair and attractive appearance are mentioned throughout the story. She has a natural and unconscious dignity that often strikes others as aloofness. As a girl, Janie leads a sheltered and conventional life with her grandmother. She is six years old before she realizes that she is black, an event that underscores her isolation from her race and her lack of self-knowledge. Through her first two marriages she holds on to an unrealistic and unfulfilled ideal of love and happiness. In her final marriage, to Tea Cake, Janie is allowed the freedom to be herself and to love on her own terms. Marriage is the frame for Janie's movement into self-knowledge and maturity.

Tea Cake (Vergible Woods), an itinerant laborer and gambler, is Janie's third husband. Much younger than she, he overcomes her doubts with beautiful language and the expectation that Janie will be herself. He takes a willing Janie into the prosperous farming region of the Everglades to pick beans. He is driven mad by rabies after being bitten by a dog during a hurricane, and Janie shoots him in self-defense.

Nanny, Janie's maternal grandmother, is a former slave who wants only security for her granddaughter. Her life both during and after slavery has been hard; her daughter is the product of rape and her granddaughter the result of a particularly brutal rape that drives Janie's mother away in shame. Nanny lives with Janie for many years in the home of her white employer, the Washburn family. With their help Nanny buys land and a house for herself and Janie. When she discovers seventeen-year-old Janie engaged in an innocent first kiss, she insists that it is time for her to marry Logan Killicks, who will, Nanny thinks, protect her from sexual and economic hardship. Love, in Nanny's experience, is "de very prong all us black women gits hung on." Nanny dies believing that money or good white people are a black woman's only protection in life.

Logan Killicks is Janie's first husband. He is much older and owns 60 acres and a house. He loves Janie and is kind to her, but he cannot understand or respond to her romantic ideas in either a mental or a physical way. Killicks is dependable and boring to a young girl dreaming of love. He realizes that Janie does not love him and tries to subdue her spirit by making her do farm labor. She rebels and runs away with Joe Starks.

Joe Starks (Jody), Janie's second husband, is an ambitious entrepreneur who takes Janie to Eatonville, a "colored" town ready for development. Soon after the wedding, his talk of love turns to talk of commerce and he buys Janie the best of everything. Janie becomes one of Jody's possessions. He insists that she sell goods at their store or at the post office and that she wear a "head-rag" to cover her hair, which men love to look at. He forbids her to participate in the storytelling that she loves, and he belittles her intelligence at every opportunity. His death releases Janie. She returns to their house, in Eatonville, after the death of Tea Cake.

Pheoby Watson is Janie's best friend, her only woman friend, whom she meets in Eatonville. They love and trust each other, and it is to Pheoby that Janie confides her problems and narrates her story.

Summary and Analysis

The **first chapter** of Zora Neale Hurston's *Their Eyes Were Watching God* begins with a description of male struggle: "Ships at a distance have every man's wish on board. For some they come in with the tide. For others they sail forever on the horizon, never out of sight, never landing until the Watcher turns his eyes away in resignation, his dreams mocked to death by Time. That is the life of men." In a different, less metaphorical voice we confront Hurston's answer to this voice, the construction of a female authorial and narrative voice: "Now, women forget all those things they don't want to remember, and remember everything they don't want to forget. The dream is the truth. Then they act and do things accordingly." The story begins. As if to confirm this refiguration of the male text "a woman" returns from burying "the bloated; the sudden dead" at "the beginning of this," a woman's story. In black dialect and lush metaphor, Hurston's narrative evokes an idea of the black woman as individual and as storyteller.

Described through the critical eyes and mouths of a Florida town (a black community called Eatonville, as we will later learn), the protagonist, Janie Starks, is forty years old; she had left town in a blue satin dress; her husband had died and was presumed to have left her money; she had taken up with another man (all wonder what *he* did with her money); and she refuses to "stay in her class." Pheoby Watson brings Janie a dinner of "mulatto rice"; they have been friends since Janie came to Eatonville. Although Hurston has been criticized by many modern black critics and writers for her use of what is called black English, the dialect creates for the reader an intimacy reserved only for the closest of friends. Overhearing the conversation between Janie and Pheoby, we are initiated into the novel's world. Janie reveals to us that she has been gone a year and a half and to Pheoby that "Tea Cake is gone. . . . Down in the Everglades there, down on the muck." The women sit on Janie's back porch and Janie tells her story to Pheoby.

In the **second chapter** the novel reveals itself to be a bildungsroman, a story about one's passage from childhood to maturity. We see events primarily through Janie's eyes. "Janie saw her life like a great tree in leaf with the things suffered, things enjoyed, things done and undone. Dawn and doom was in the branches." The motif of the tree, a recurrent thematic element, will recur throughout the novel.

Janie was raised by Nanny, her grandmother, first in the home of Nanny's white employer and, later, in a house Nanny buys. In this chapter Janie recalls two events that define her childhood. The first concerns a photograph, the second, a first kiss. Janie is photographed with a group of white children, and she cannot see herself in the finished picture. "Dat's you, Alphabet, don't you know yo' ownself?" a white woman laughs. For Janie, the realization that she is "colored," and not "just like de rest," is an epiphany, a profound revelation that changes her stance toward the world. Her "colored" schoolmates tease her about "livin' in de white folks' backyard" and refuse to play with her, so Nanny buys a house and land for the two of them.

"Shiftless" Johnny Taylor comes later, transformed by her youthful perceptions ("the golden dust of pollen had beglamored his rags and her eyes"); she kisses him. She names this moment the beginning of her "conscious life." Nanny sees the boy "lacerating her Janie with a kiss" and knows that she is no longer the strongest influence in Janie's life; she is like a "foundation of ancient power that no longer mattered." We may interpret this enigmatic allusion in many ways. Most immediately it suggests that the power of a mother to protect her daughter—or a grandmother her granddaughter—ends when the girl turns to the world of men, outside the home where the old woman "no longer matter[s]." Nanny insists that seventeen-year-old Janie marry a prosperous but dull farmer, Logan Killicks, who will protect her from the vulnerabilities of her gender and class. But, she tells Janie that even Logan will not protect her from some things, now that she has left Nanny's home. Nanny offers a parable about a further division of gender within race: "De nigger woman is de mule uh de world so fur as Ah can see. Ah been prayin' fuh it tuh be different wid you." A

21

former slave, her own daughter the product of rape, she wants only to see her granddaughter safe within marriage.

In **chapter three** Janie marries Killicks, hopeful that marriage might somehow "compel love like the sun the day." It does not, and she turns to Nanny for advice. In Nanny's experience, love has always demanded sacrifice—a woman's sacrifice. She advises Janie to be patient, but Janie feels for Killicks only that "some folks never was meant to be loved and he's one of 'em." Within a month Nanny dies.

In **chapter four**, while Killicks is away, Joe (Jody) Starks, a well-dressed, "cityfied" man, stops and asks for a drink. More worldly than Janie, he represents to her the possibilities of "change and chance." She leaves Killicks and marries Joe Starks. The reader should consider the implications of marriage in this novel: Nanny had believed that marriage offered protection to her granddaughter. But the bond seems here to have no legal significance. What sort of protection is possible? Janie's romantic dreams of "flower dust and spring time" cannot endure, as the reader knows, but Hurston's novel is neither an allegory nor a morality tale, and the lessons embedded in the text are not so simple. Joe Starks promises to be "a big ruler of things with her reaping the benefits."

In the **fifth chapter** Joe and Janie arrive at Eatonville, a "colored town," where Starks will establish himself as a civic figure and entrepreneur. Starks astonishes the sleepy town when he pays cash for 200 acres of land, builds a general store, sells lots to newcomers, and establishes a post office. The idea of "[u]h colored man sittin' up in uh post office" seems preposterous to some, but others sense possibility and progress.

As Starks rightly predicts, the store becomes the natural meeting place for the town. He has Janie work in the store as a symbol and proof of his rank: "She must look on herself as the bell-cow, the other women were the gang." Her silk dress and long, beautiful hair contrasts with the humble percale and calico dresses and occasional "head-rags" of the townswomen. In a scene that draws upon the ideals of ancient Greek oratory, a townsman attempting a panegyric to the Starks is stopped by another who insists that he has forgotten a vital component of this type of speech: He must compare them to the biblical Isaac and Rebecca. All agree that "[i]t was sort of pitiful for Tony not to know he couldn't make a speech without saying that." They appoint Joe Starks mayor and ask for a speech from Janie. Starks intervenes and prevents her from speaking because "[s]he's a woman and her place is in de home." That night he strides home, "invested with his new dignity," and Janie follows, disappointed in her husband, "the bloom off of things."

As Joe distinguishes himself as landowner, mayor, postmaster, and civic visionary, the Starks become separate from the others by class. Many of their neighbors are jealous, feeling somehow as if "they had been taken advantage of. Like things had been kept from them. . . . It was bad enough for white people, but when one of your own color could be so different. . . . [i]t was like seeing your sister turn into a 'gator. A familiar strangeness."

More than the commerce at the store Janie enjoys the conversation, "[w]hen the people sat around on the porch and passed around the pictures of their thoughts for others to see." In **chapter six** "the case of Matt Bonner's yellow mule" becomes a metaphor for the community. The men who sit on the porch of the store never miss a chance to ridicule Matt and entertain themselves with "stories about how poor the brute was; his age; his evil disposition and his latest caper." Janie imagines her own stories about the mule, but Joe forbids her to take part. Joe may believe that her duties in the post office and in the store are her "privileges," but, to Janie, they are "the rock she [is] battered against." He forbids Janie to show her beautiful hair, admired by the men, and insists she wear a "head-rag," which she hates. He cannot admit his jealousy, and Janie compares his reticence to "the matter of the yellow mule."

Joe Starks buys the mule from Matt for five dollars, not to put it to work but so that the animal can rest at last. The men and Janie are impressed with such a noble act, "no everyday thought." Like Abraham Lincoln freeing the slaves, the power to free the mule makes Joe "lak uh king uh something." When the mule eventually dies, all work is suspended. Janie watches from the doorway of the store as "the carcass move[s] off with the town" to the swamp where they "[mock] everything human in death." Joe acts as preacher to speak of "mule-angels flying around . . . [and] no Matt Bonner with plow lines and halters to come in and corrupt." The "sisters get . . . mock-happy" and the vultures circle, waiting for the carcass. The vultures move in, and enact a *mise en abyme*, a play within a play, about the townspeople in the greater human society. When the crowd finally leaves, the vultures proceed with mock-human ceremony. None may feast on the carcass until their leader arrives. The "Parson," with all decorum, chants over the mule, "What killed this man?" and the chorus responds, incomprehensibly, "Bare, bare fat." He ritually picks out the eyes and all may then eat.

"The years took all the fight out of Janie's face," and, in the **seventh chapter**, at age thirty-five, she feels beaten down by the routine of the store and by her marriage: "She got nothing from Jody except what money could buy, and she was giving away what she didn't value." Tensions grow between the two as Joe becomes increasingly sensitive to the contrast between his wife's youthful beauty and his own physical and spiritual aging beyond his fifty years. His body begins to fail him. He frequently speaks of Janie as if she were no longer young. But "[f]or the first time she could see a man's head naked of its skull. Saw cunning thoughts race in and out through the caves and promontories of his mind long before they darted out of the tunnel of his mouth. . . . She just measured out a little time for him and set it aside to wait." Joe humiliates Janie by reproaching her for improperly cutting a piece of tobacco for a customer and, for the first time, Janie challenges her husband in public. "When you pull down yo' britches you look lak de change uh life," she angrily responds. The men in the store laugh and "Joe Starks realize[s] all the meanings and his vanity [bleeds] like a flood. Janie had robbed him of his illusion of irresistible maleness that all men cherish, which was terrible." Joe strikes Janie and drives her from the store.

Joe Starks's death, in **chapter eight**, marks another turning point in Janie's life. She sits alone at his deathbed and pities this man whom she had married twenty years earlier. Although he "had been hard on her and others . . . life had mishandled him too." Janie removes her head rag and lets down her still-beautiful hair. At once widowed and released, Janie opens the window and announces to the waiting townspeople, "Mah husband is gone from me." After an elaborate funeral in **chapter nine**, Janie returns home and burns all her head rags. Self-interested men come from great distances to offer to advise her, telling her, "Uh woman by herself is uh pitiful thing." But Janie likes "being lonesome for a change" and notes that the only difference between her and the many other women like her is that they are poor and she is prosperous. She remarks to Pheoby that "mourning oughtn't tuh last no longer'n grief."

One afternoon, when Janie is alone in the store in **chapter ten**, a stranger, who identifies himself by the end of the chapter as "Vergible Woods. . . . Tea Cake for short," enters and greets her by name, "Good evenin', Mis' Starks." He is from Orlando, seven miles away; he buys cigarettes, and Janie "look[s] him over and [gets] little thrills from every one of his good points." He challenges her to a game of checkers, a popular pastime in the store. She has never learned to play because no one had expected her to do so, until now. When Janie closes the store that evening, she is concerned about Tea Cake's long walk back to Orlando. In an exchange that foreshadows her physical and spiritual journey with Tea Cake, he tells her "Ah'm seen women walk further'n dat. You could too, if yuh had it tuh do." He walks her home, and she thinks, "Tea Cake wasn't strange. Seemed as if she had known him all her life."

In **chapter eleven**, Janie mentally compiles a list of reasons why Tea Cake is an unsuitable match for her: He is "around twenty-five and here she was around forty," he doesn't seem prosperous and may be interested in taking her money, and he is "probably the kind of man who lived with various women but never married." She decided to "treat him so cold if he ever did foot the place that he'd be sure not to come hanging around there again." When Tea Cake returns to the store a week later, her resolve to spurn him dissolves. Tea Cake remains with Janie after everyone goes home, and at midnight he takes her fishing. Janie enjoys feeling "like a child breaking rules," and they return to her house at dawn. She "[has] to smuggle Tea Cake out by the back gate . . . like some great secret she was keeping from the town." It is a secret impossible to protect. The difference in their ages worries her, and she suspects he may think her a fool. Warmed by his profession of love, one moment she feels "fit up like a transfiguration," only to feel doubt the next. Tea Cake insists that age "got nuthin' tuh do wid love." He is different from any man she has known, "a glance from God." All Janie's uncertainties vanish as they prepare to attend the Sunday school picnic the next day. "You got de keys to de kingdom," Tea Cake tells her, declaring both his love and his commitment to Janie.

Janie's public appearance with Tea Cake at the Sunday school picnic provokes intense disapproval and gossip among the townspeople. "It was after the picnic that the town began to notice things and got mad," begins **chapter twelve**. Janie, as the widow of Joe Starks, is a symbol of accomplishment and high class in Eatonville. Tea Cake is a drifter and an outsider. Their catalog of suspicions and complaints about the pair is long. Nothing escapes scrutiny, from her new dresses and differently combed hair to the certainty that Tea Cake is only after Joe Starks's money. Janie confides in Pheoby Watson that Tea Cake is her chance for happiness, a chance she is ready to take: "Some of dese mornin's and it won't be long, you goin' tuh wake up callin' me and Ah'll be gone."

In **chapter thirteen** Janie leaves Eatonville with Tea Cake. Those few townspeople who see her board the train for Jacksonville early in the morning note that she "looked good, but she had no business to do it. It was hard to love a woman that always made you feel so wishful." Tea Cake meets Janie on her arrival, and they immediately get married. On Pheoby's advice, Janie had pinned two hundred dollars inside her shirt, because "things might not turn out like she thought."

Tea Cake and Janie move into a boardinghouse in Jacksonville, and that morning he leaves early to "get some fish to fry for breakfast." By noon he has not returned, and Janie discovers that Tea Cake has taken her two hundred dollars. She remembers another woman, a widow at fifty-two, with "a good home and insurance money." She had love affairs with men and teenage boys, spent all her "ready cash" on them, and was abandoned by each "as soon as their wants were satisfied"; then came a man who persuaded her to sell her house and go to Tampa with him. She was "[a]s sure as Janie had been" when she boarded the train, only to be abandoned by this new man and left to beg in the streets. But Janie is not the fool that the notorious widow was; she has "ten dollars in her pocket and twelve hundred in the bank" and her house in Eatonville.

Tea Cake returns the next day with declarations of love—and a story about Janie's two hundred dollars. He had "spied the money while he was tying his tie" and pocketed it to count it later. "He never had had his hand on so much money before in his life, so he made up his mind to see how it felt to be a millionaire," and he threw a party to impress old friends and new with his affluence. The account of the party, with an anecdote about ugly women paid not to attend, a fist fight, and Tea Cake retrieving his guitar from the pawnshop converge and collide to defuse Janie's anger. He promises to repay her by playing dice with the workers who get paid "dis comin' Saturday at de railroad yards."

On Saturday, Tea Cake buys "a new switch-blade knife and two decks of star-back playing cards" and leaves for the railroad yards. Tea Cake returns at dawn, cut in a knife fight when he tried to leave the game; he has won back Janie's two hundred dollars and much more. He insists that she take the two hundred and deposit it in the bank with her own money. He will provide for her from now on, without her assistance. "When Ah ain't got nothin' you don't git nothin'," he tells her. This is "all right" with Janie. As they fall asleep, Tea Cake tells her they are "goin' on de muck . . . down in de Everglades . . . where dey raise all dat cane and stringbeans and tomatuhs. Folks don't do nothin' down dere but make money and fun and foolishness." As Janie watches him in his sleep, she feels "a self-crushing love, . . . [and] her soul crawl[s] out from its hiding place."

The richness of the land in the Everglades astonishes Janie in **chapter fourteen**, and the people seem as wild as the lush weeds and wild cane. Tea Cake has come to plant and pick beans and to roll dice. "Between de beans and de dice Ah can't lose," he says. He finds a good job with "houses fuh de first ones dat git dere." He teaches Janie to shoot, advising her that "Even if you didn't never find no game, it's always some trashy rascal dat needs uh good killin'." (Is this remark a foreshadowing of events or is it an allusion to how Tea Cake might be judged by those who do not love him?)

All the workers make money and spend it easily; "[n]ext month and next year were other times. No need to mix them up with the present." Tea Cake's house becomes "a magnet, the unauthorized center of the 'job.'" His guitar, his humor, and his ambition draw people to him. People come every night to Tea Cake's house to hear him "pick the box" (play the guitar), to tell stories, and to gamble. Janie laughs to herself, wondering, "What if Eatonville could see her now in her blue denim overalls and heavy shoes?" The men hold "big arguments" like those she used to hear on the porch of the store. But here, "she could listen and laugh and even talk some herself if she wanted to. She got so she could tell big stories herself from listening to the rest."

In **chapter fifteen** Janie learns "what it [feels] like to be jealous" when a young girl lures Tea Cake away from the crowd with games and teasing to make him chase her. Janie thinks that Tea Cake does not resist the girl strongly enough, and jealousy and a "little seed of fear [begin] growing into a tree." She discovers Tea Cake and the girl "struggling" together on the ground between rows of cane, and later, in a violent confrontation with Tea Cake, she believes his claim that he had never wanted the girl. He assures Janie that only she is "something tuh make uh man forgit tuh git old and forgit tuh die."

The picking season ends and most of the workers and families leave. In **chapter sixteen** Tea Cake and Janie decide to stay and work again the next season. Humor and pathos converge in this chapter in the figure of Mrs. Turner, a "milky sort of woman . . . [who] must have been conscious of her pelvis because she kept it stuck out in front of her so she could always see it." As far as Mrs. Turner is concerned, however, her shape and her features are just fine. "To her way of thinking [her Caucasian features] set her aside from Negroes." She approves of Janie's "coffee-and-cream complexion and her luxurious hair" but despises Tea Cake because of his dark skin. Negroes are Mrs. Turner's "dis-favorite subject." In the face of the woman's earnest fanaticism, Janie can think of nothing to say. Janie, conscious of all Nanny had taught her, thinks the woman's speech is "sacrilege" and decides to say no more. At last, Mrs. Turner leaves and Janie finds Tea Cake sitting in the kitchen with his head between his hands.

Chapter sixteen marks the most prominent authorial intrusion into the narrative. Hurston gives to the reader an analysis of Mrs. Turner that Janie would not be able to construct: "Mrs. Turner, like all other believers had built an altar to the unattainable—Caucasian characteristics for all. . . . The physical impossibilities in no way injured faith. That was the mystery and mysteries are the chores of gods. . . . And when she was with Janie she had a feeling of transmutation, as if she herself had become whiter and with straighter hair and she hated Tea Cake first for his defilement of divinity and next for his telling mockery of her." Hurston resumes the story of Janie and Tea Cake with the return of the old crowd for the new season in **chapter seventeen**.

When Mrs. Turner introduces her light-skinned brother to Janie, in an attempt to separate Janie from Tea Cake, Tea Cake has a "brainstorm" about how to assert his possession of her: He "slap[s] her around a bit to show [the Turners] he was boss." The event is the talk of the fields the next day. The men think Tea Cake is a "lucky man" to have a woman who will let him beat her without fighting back. He brags that Janie, although she has money in the bank, will stay "on de muck" in the fields or wherever Tea Cake wants to be. The incident of Tea Cake's slapping Janie disappears into the story. We never learn Janie's response.

The next payday the men get drunk and, "to take uh rest from our women folks' cookin'," the "familiar crowd" eats dinner at Mrs. Turner's "eating house." Tea Cake, while subtly encouraging a fight among the drunken patrons, acts apparently to stop the turmoil. Another man proclaims Mrs. Turner "more nicer than anybody else on de muck"; she beams on him in approval. But the fight escalates until "dishes and tables beg[i]n to crash." Afterward, the establishment a ruin, Mrs. Turner angrily tells her husband that they are "goin' back tuh Miami where folks is civilized." Tea Cake has succeeded in driving the Turners away.

In **chapter eighteen** Janie is home alone one afternoon. Large bands of Seminole Indians are steadily moving inland, and she learns from them that a hurricane is coming. The people at last believe the signs of danger when "the palm and banana trees beg[i]n that long distance talk with rain." Buzzards gather and stay above the clouds, but Tea Cake refuses to leave because "de white folks ain't gone nowhere" and "de money's too good on the muck." Those who stay wait out the hurricane in their shanties, "their eyes straining against crude walls and their souls asking if He meant to measure their puny might against His. They seemed to be staring at the dark, but their eyes were watching God."

Tea Cake and Janie collect their cash and their insurance papers and wade into the hip-deep water in the yard, amid fast-moving debris. The 10-foot dike wall breeched, Lake Okeechobee leaves its bed in a 200-mile-an-hour wind. Tea Cake and Janie swim until they "[gain] the fill" where many others also walk, "calling out names hopefully and hopelessly." When Tea Cake is too tired to walk any farther, he "stretch[es] long side of the road to rest" and Janie "spread[s] herself between him and the wind." She is blown into the water when she tries to catch a piece of tarpaper roofing to cover Tea Cake. She grabs the tail of a cow swimming near her, a "massive built dog . . . on her shoulders." As the dog roars and lunges for Janie, Tea Cake dives into the water and seizes the dog, his knife open to kill it. But Tea Cake is exhausted, and the dog bites him on the face before dying. Tea Cake and Janie reach Palm Beach in the aftermath of the storm. Janie will never forget the eyes of that dog: "He wuzn't nothin' all over but pure hate. Wonder where he come from?"

Tea Cake is anxious to leave Palm Beach in **chapter nineteen**. But first, he must find work. Two white men with rifles conscript him into "a small army . . . to bury the dead." The white corpses get coffins; the black corpses get quicklime. He convinces Janie that they must return to the 'Glades. Hurston again intrudes into the mouths of her characters to instruct the reader on racism: "De ones de white man know is nice colored folks. De ones he don't know is bad niggers," Janie observes to Tea Cake. The reader may find it difficult to believe this conversation about something they already know is taking place during a hellish crisis.

They return to the Everglades, where there is plenty of work clearing debris to make way for new buildings. Tea Cake buys another rifle and a pistol. He is a little jealous of Janie's skill with a rifle but proud that he has taught her so well. He soon develops rabies as a result of the dog bite during the hurricane. The disease has progressed too far for medical help, and Janie wishes she had drowned before Tea Cake grabbed the dog: "Tea Cake, the son of Evening Sun, had to die for loving her," she thinks. Suspicions and jealousy become madness in Tea Cake's diseased mind and he levels the pistol at Janie's breast, snapping it once. Janie instinctively brings the rifle around to scare him. He levels the gun at her again, as if "[t]he fiend in him must kill and Janie was the only thing living he saw." They shoot at each other simultaneously, and Tea Cake is killed.

Janie is briefly jailed on charges of murder. Because of the circumstances of the killing, she is represented, tried, and acquitted (by white men) within hours. She stays at a boardinghouse that night and overhears men talking: "Well, you know whut dey say 'uh white man and uh nigger woman is de freest thing on earth.' Dey do as dey please." Janie buries Tea Cake in Palm Beach.

In **chapter twenty** the narrative returns to the porch, Janie soaking her tired feet in a pan of water and Pheoby listening to her story. Pheoby goes home to her husband, Sam, vowing to make him take her fishing, and Janie retires to her bedroom. Tea Cake is not dead to Janie: "He could never be dead until she herself had finished feeling and thinking." The killing of Tea Cake suggests that a black woman has an explosive power to claim her voice and to tell her story.

Critical Views

Their Eyes has often been described as a novel about a woman in a folk community, but it might be more accurately described as a novel about a woman outside of the folk community. And while feminists have been eager to seize upon this text as an expression of female power, I think it is a novel that represents women's exclusion from power, particularly from the power of oral speech. . . . Janie's image of herself as a blossom waiting to be pollinated by a bee transforms her figuratively and literally into the space in which men's action may occur.[9] She waits for an answer and the answer appears in the form of two men, both of whom direct Janie's life and the action of the plot. Janie at least resists her first husband, Logan, but once Jody takes her to Eatonville, he controls her life as well as the narrative. He buys the land, builds the town, makes Janie tie up her hair, and prescribes her relationship with the rest of the town. We know that Hurston means for Janie to free herself from male domination, but Hurston's language, as much as Jody's behavior, signifies Janie's status as an object. Janie's arrival in Eatonville is described through the eyes and speech of the men on the front porch. Jody joins the men, but Janie is seen "through the bedroom window getting settled." Not only are Janie and the other women barred from participation in the ceremonies and rituals of the community, but they become the objects of the sessions on the porch, included in the men's tale-telling as the butt of their jokes, or their flattery, or their scorn. The experience of having one's body become an object to be looked at is considered so demeaning that when it happens to a man, it figuratively transforms him into a woman. When Janie launches her most devastating attack on Jody in front of all the men in the store, she tells him not to talk about her looking old because "When you pull down yo' britches you look lak

33

de change uh life." Since the "change of life" ordinarily refers to a woman's menopause, Janie is signifying that Jody, like a woman, is subject to the humiliation of exposure. Now that he is the object of the gaze, Jody realizes that other men will "look" on him with pity: "Janie had robbed him of his illusion of irresistible maleness that all men cherish."

Eventually Janie does speak, and, interestingly, her first speech, on behalf of women, is a commentary on the limitations of a male-dominated society.

> Sometimes God gits familiar wid us womenfolks too and talks His inside business. He told me how surprised He was 'bout y'all turning out so smart after Him makin' yuh different; and how surprised y'all is goin' tuh be if you ever find out you don't know half as much 'bout us as you think you do.

Speech does not lead Janie to power, however, but to self-division and to further acquiescence in her status as object. As her marriage to Jody deteriorates she begins to observe herself: "one day she sat and watched the shadows of herself going about tending store and prostrating itself before Jody, while all the time she herself sat under a shady tree with the wind blowing through her hair and her clothes." . . .

Even after Janie acquires the power of speech that allows her to stand up to Jody, Hurston continues to objectify her so that she does not take action. Immediately after Jody's death she goes to the looking glass where, she tells us, she has told her girl self to wait for her, and there she discovers that a handsome woman has taken her place. She tears off the kerchief Jody has forced her to wear and lets down her plentiful hair: "The weight, the length, the glory was there. She took careful stock of herself, then combed her hair and tied it back up again." In her first moment of independence Janie is not seen as autonomous subject but again as visual object, "seeing herself seeing herself," draping before herself that "hidden mystery" that attracts men and makes her superior to women. Note that when she turns to the mirror, it is not to experience her own sensual pleasure in her hair. She does not tell us how her hair felt to her—did it tingle at the roots? Did she shiver with delight?—no, she takes stock of herself, makes an assessment of herself. What's in the mirror that she cannot experience without it: that imaginary other whom the mirror represents, looking on in judgment, recording, not her own sensations but the way others see her.

Barbara Johnson's reading of *Their Eyes* suggests that once Janie is able to identify the split between her inside and outside selves, incorporating and articulating her own sense of self-division, she develops an increasing ability to speak.[10] I have come to different conclusions: that Hurston continues to subvert Janie's voice, that in crucial places where we need to hear her speak she is curiously silent, that even when Hurston sets out to explore Janie's internal consciousness, her internal speech, what we actually hear are the voices of men. Once Tea Cake enters the narrative his name and his voice are heard nearly twice as often as Janie's. He walks into Janie's life with a guitar and a grin and tells her, "Honey since you loose me and gimme privilege tuh tell yuh all about mahself. Ah'll tell yuh." And from then on it is Tea Cake's tale, the only reason for Janie's account of her life to Pheoby being to vindicate Tea Cake's name. Insisting on Tea Cake's innocence as well as his central place in her story, Janie tells Pheoby, "Teacake ain't wasted no money of mine, and he ain't left me for no young gal, neither. He give me every consolation in the world. He'd tell 'em so too, if he was here. If he wasn't gone."

As many feminist critics have pointed out, women do get silenced, even in texts by women, and there are critical places in *Their Eyes* where Janie's voice needs to be heard and is not, places where we would expect her as the subject of the story to speak. Perhaps the most stunning silence in the text occurs after Tea Cake beats Janie. The beating is seen entirely through the eyes of the male community, while Janie's reaction is never given. Tea Cake becomes the envy of the other men for having a woman whose flesh is so tender that one can see every place she's been hit. Sop-de-Bottom declares in awe, "wouldn't Ah love tuh whip uh tender woman lak Janie!" Janie is silent, so thoroughly repressed in this section that all that remains of her is what Tea Cake and the other men desire.

Passages that are supposed to represent Janie's interior consciousness begin by marking some internal change in Janie, then gradually or abruptly shift so that a male character takes Janie's place as the subject of the discourse; at the conclusion of these passages, ostensibly devoted to the revelation of Janie's interior life, the male voice predominates. Janie's life just before and after Jody's death is a fertile period for such self-reflection, but Hurston does not focus the attention of the text on Janie even in these significant turning points in Janie's life. In the long paragraph that tells us how she has changed in the six months after Jody's death, we are told that Janie talked and laughed in the store at times and was happy except for the store. To solve the problem of the store she hires Hezikiah "who was the best imitation of Joe that his seventeen years could make." At this point, the paragraph shifts its focus from Janie and her growing sense of independence to Hezikiah and his imitation of Jody, describing Hezikiah in a way that evokes Jody's presence and obliterates Janie. We are told at the end of the paragraph, in tongue-in-cheek humor, that because "managing stores and women storeowners was trying on a man's nerves," Hezikiah "needed to take a drink of liquor now and then to keep up." Thus Janie is not only removed as the subject of this passage but is subsumed under the male-defined category of worrisome women. Even the much-celebrated description of Janie's discovery of her split selves: "She had an inside and an outside now and suddenly she knew how not to mix them" represents her internal life as divided between two men: her outside self exists for Joe and her inside self she is "saving up" for "some man she had never seen."[11]

Notes
9. Teresa De Lauretis, *Alice Doesn't: Feminism, Semiotics, Cinema* (Bloomington: Indiana University Press, 1984), 143. De Lauretis notes that the movement of narrative discourse specifies and produces the masculine position as that of mythical subject and the feminine position as mythical obstacle, or, simply "the space in which that movement occurs."

10. I am indebted to Barbara Johnson for this insight which she suggested when I presented an early version of this paper to her class of Afro-American women writers at Harvard in the fall of 1985. I was struck by her comment that Jody's vulnerability makes him like a woman and therefore subject to this kind of attack.

11. Barbara Johnson, "Metaphor, Metonymy, and Voice in *Their Eyes Were Watching God*," in *Black Literature and Literary Theory*, ed. Henry Louis Gates, Jr. (New York: Methuen, 1984), 204–219. Johnson's essay probes very carefully the relation between Janie's ability to speak and her ability to recognize her own self-division. Once Janie is able "to assume and articulate the incompatible forces involved in her own division," she begins to achieve an authentic voice. Arguing for a more literal reading of *Their Eyes*, I maintain that we hear precious little of Janie's voice even after she makes this pronouncement of knowing that she has "an inside and an outside self." A great deal of the "voice" of the text is devoted to the men in the story even after Janie's discovery of self-division.

HENRY LOUIS GATES JR. CONTRASTS ZORA NEALE HURSTON WITH RICHARD WRIGHT AND RALPH ELLISON

Zora Neale Hurston is the first writer that our generation of black and feminist critics has brought into the canon, or perhaps I should say the canons. For Hurston is now a cardinal figure in the Afro-American canon, the feminist canon, and the canon of American fiction, especially as our readings of her work become increasingly close readings, which Hurston's texts sustain delightfully. The curious aspect of the widespread critical attention being shown to Hurston's texts is that so many critics embracing such a diversity of theoretical approaches seem to find something new at which to marvel in her texts.

My own method of reading *Their Eyes Were Watching God* stems fundamentally from the debates over modes of representation, over theories of mimesis, which as I have suggested form such a crucial part of the history of Afro-American literature and its theory. Mimetic principles can be both implicitly and explicitly ideological, and the explication of Hurston's rhetorical strategy, which I shall attempt below,

37

is no exception. I wish to read *Their Eyes* in such a way as to move from the broadest notion of *what* it thematizes through an ever-tighter spiral of *how* it thematizes, that is, its rhetorical strategies. I shall attempt to show that Hurston's text not only cleared a rhetorical space for the narrative strategies that Ralph Ellison would render so deftly in *Invisible Man*, but also that Hurston's text is the first example in our tradition of "the speakerly text," by which I mean a text whose rhetorical strategy is designed to represent an oral literary tradition, designed "to emulate the phonetic, grammatical, and lexical patterns of actual speech and produce the 'illusion of oral narration.'"[19] The speakerly text is that text in which all other structural elements seem to be devalued, as important as they remain to the telling of the tale, because the narrative strategy signals attention to its own importance, an importance which would seem to be the privileging of oral speech and its inherent linguistic features. Whereas Toomer's *Cane* draws upon the black oral voice essentially as a different voice from the narrator's, as a repository of socially distinct, contrapuntal meanings and beliefs, a speakerly text would seem primarily to be oriented toward imitating one of the numerous forms of oral narration to be found in classical Afro-American vernacular literature.

Obviously, I am concerned with what we traditionally think of as matters of voice. "Voice" here connotes not only traditional definitions of "point of view," a crucial matter in the reading of *Their Eyes*, but also the linguistic presence of a literary tradition that exists for us as a written text primarily because of the work of sociolinguists and anthropologists such as Hurston. I am concerned in this chapter to discuss the representation of what we might think of as the voice of the black oral tradition—represented here as direct speech—as well as with Hurston's use of free indirect discourse as the rhetorical analogue to the text's metaphors of inside and outside, so fundamental to the depiction of Janie's quest for consciousness, her very quest to become a speaking black subject. Just as we have begun to think of Hurston as an artist whose texts relate to those of Jean Toomer and Sterling

A. Brown, let us round out our survey of the tradition by comparing Hurston's concept of voice with that of Richard Wright and Ralph Ellison.

In *American Hunger* (1977), which along with *Black Boy* (1945) comprises the full text of an autobiography he initially called "The Horror and the Glory," Richard Wright succinctly outlines his idea of the ironic relationship between the individual black talent and an Afro-American cultural tradition ravaged and laid waste to by an omnipresent and irresistible white racism:

> What could I dream of that had the barest possibility of coming true? I could think of nothing. And, slowly, it was upon exactly that nothingness that my mind began to dwell, that constant sense of wanting without having, of being hated without reason. A dim notion of what life meant to a Negro in America was coming to consciousness in me, not in terms of external events, lynchings, Jim Crowism, and the endless brutalities, but in terms of crossed-up feelings, of psyche pain. I sensed that Negro life was a sprawling land of unconscious suffering, and that there were but few Negroes who knew the meaning of their lives, who could tell their [own] story.[20]

Wright, as both of his autobiographies seem intent on claiming, certainly counted himself among those few Negroes who could tell not only their own story but also the woeful tale of their pathetic, voiceless black countrymen. If they were signs of the "horror," then his articulated escape was meant to be our "glory."

In his autobiographies and novels, Wright evolved a curious and complex myth of origins of self and race. Whereas a large part of the black autobiographical tradition, as exemplified by Frederick Douglass's three autobiographies, generally depicts a resplendent self as representative of possibilities denied systematically to one's voiceless fellow blacks, Wright's class of ideal individual black selves seems to have included only Wright. *Black Boy*, for example, charts how the boy, Dick, through the key texts of naturalism, gave a shape and a purpose to an exceptional inherent nobility of spirit which emerges from within the chaotic depths of the black cultural maelstrom. Wright's humanity is achieved only at the expense of his fellow blacks, pitiable victims of the pathology of slavery and racial segregation who surround and suffocate him. Indeed, Wright wills this especial self into being through the agency of contrast: the sensitive, healthy part is foregrounded against a determined, defeated black whole. He is a noble black savage, in the ironic tradition of Oroonoko and film characters played by Sidney Poitier—the exception, not the rule.

For Ralph Ellison, Wright's notion of the self and its relation to black culture seemed unduly costly. Indeed, it is this dark and brooding fiction of black culture against which both Ellison and James Baldwin railed, drawing upon a rich body of tropes and rhetorical strategies prefigured, among other places, in Hurston's fictions and critical writings. It is this fiction of obliteration that created the great divide in black literature, a fissure first rendered apparent in the late thirties in an extended debate between Hurston and Wright.

The Hurston–Wright debate, staged not only in the lyrical shape of *Their Eyes Were Watching God* (1937) against the naturalism of *Native Son* (1940) but also in reviews of each other's books, turns between two poles of a problematic of representation—between what is represented and what represents, between the signifier and the signified. Theirs are diametrically opposed notions of the internal structure of the sign, the very sign of blackness.

Hurston rather self-consciously defined her theory of the novel against that received practice of realism which Wright would attempt to revitalize in *Native Son*. Hurston thought that Wright stood at the center of "the sobbing school of Negrohood who hold that nature somehow has given them a low down dirty deal."[21] Against Wright's idea of psychological destruction and chaos, Hurston framed a counternotion which the repressed and conservative maternal figure of *Their Eyes* articulates: "[It] wasn't for me to fulfill my dreams of whut a woman oughta be and to do. Dat's one of de hold-backs of slavery. But nothing can't stop you from wishin'. You can't beat nobody down so low till you can rob 'em of they will." The sign of this transcendent self would be the shaping of a strong, self-reflective voice: "Ah wanted to preach a great sermon about colored women sittin' on high, but they wasn't no pulpit for me. Freedom found me widh a baby daughter in mah arms, so Ah said Ah'd take a broom and a cook-pot and throw up a highway through de wilderness for her. She would expound what Ah felt. But somehow she got lost off a de highway and next thing Ah knowed here you was in de world. So whilst Ah was tendin' you of nights Ah said Ah'd save de text for you."[22] Hurston revoices this notion of the articulating subject in her autobiography, *Dust Tracks on the Road* (1942), in a curious account of her mother's few moments before death: "Her mouth was slightly open, but her breathing took up so much of her strength that she could not talk. But, she looked at me, or so I felt, to speak for her. She depended on me for a voice."[23] We can begin to understand how far apart Hurston and Wright stand in the tradition if we compare Hurston's passage about her mother with the following passage from Wright's *Black Boy*, a deathbed revision of Hurston's passage:

Once, in the night, my mother called me to her bed and told me that she could not endure the pain, that she wanted to die. I held her hand and begged her to be quiet. That night I ceased to react to my mother; my feelings were frozen.[24]

Wright explains that this event, and his mother's extended suffering, "grew into a symbol in my mind, gathering to itself all the poverty, the ignorance, the helplessness; . . . Her life set the emotional tone of my life, colored the men and women I was to meet in the future, conditioned my relation to events that had not happened, determined my attitude to situations and circumstances I had yet to face." If Hurston figures her final moments with her mother in terms of the search for a voice, then Wright, three years later, figures the significance of a similar scene as responsible for a certain "somberness of spirit that I was never to lose." No two authors in the tradition are more dissimilar than Hurston and Wright.

The narrative voice Hurston created, and her legacy to Afro-American fiction, is a lyrical and disembodied yet individual voice, from which emerges a singular longing and utterance, a transcendent, ultimately racial self, extending far beyond the merely individual. Hurston realized a resonant and authentic narrative voice that echoes and aspires to the status of the impersonality, anonymity, and authority of the black vernacular tradition, a nameless, selfless tradition, at once collective and compelling, true somehow to the unwritten text of a common blackness. For Hurston, the search for a telling form of language, indeed the search for a black literary language itself, defines the search for the self. Similarly, for Ellison, the self can emerge only through the will, as signified by the problematical attempt to write itself into being, a unique black self consolidated and rendered integral within a first-person narrative structure.

For Wright, nature was ruthless, irreducible, and ineffable. Unlike Hurston and Ellison, Wright sees fiction not as a model of reality but as a representative bit of it, a literal report of the real. Art, for Wright, always remains referential. His blackness, therefore, can never be a mere sign; it is rather the text of his great and terrible subject. Accordingly, Wright draws upon the voice of the third-person, past-tense authorial mode and various tools of empirical social science and naturalism to blend public with private experience, inner with outer history. Rarely does he relinquish what Roland Barthes calls the "proprietary consciousness," the constant sign of his presence and of some larger context, which the third-person voice inevitably entails. Rather predictably, Wright found Hurston's great novel to be "counter-revolutionary," while Hurston replied that she wrote novels "and not treatises on sociology."

Hurston, Wright, and Ellison's divergent theories of narrative structure and voice, the cardinal points of a triangle of influence, with their attendant ramifications upon the ideology of form and its relation to knowledge and power, comprise a matrix of issues to which subsequent black fictions, by definition, must respond. The rhetorical question that subsequent texts must answer remained the question which the structure of *Their Eyes* answered for Hurston: "In what voice would the Negro speak for her or himself in the language of fiction?" By discussing *Their Eyes'* topoi and figures, its depiction of the relationship among character, consciousness, and setting, and its engagement of shifting points of view, we can begin to understand how primary Hurston's rhetorical strategies remain in this compelling text.

Notes

19. I cite a definition of *skaz* deliberately, for this concept of Russian Formalism is similar to what I am calling the speakerly. See Victor Erlich, *Russian Formalism: History-Doctrine* (Mouton: The Hague, 1969), p. 238.

20. Richard Wright, *American Hunger* (New York: Harper & Row, 1979), p. 7.

21. Zora Neale Hurston, "How It Feels to Be Colored Me," *The World Tomorrow* (1928).

22. Zora Neale Hurston, *Their Eyes Were Watching God* (1937; Urbana: University of Illinois, 1978), pp. 31–32. All subsequent references are to this edition and will be given parenthetically in the text.

23. Zora Neale Hurston, *Dust Tracks on a Road: An Autobiography* (Philadelphia: J.B. Lippincott, 1942), pp. 94–95. Subsequent references will be given parenthetically.

24. Richard Wright, *Black Boy* (1945; New York: Harper & Row, 1966), p. 111.

NEAL A. LESTER ON EBONICS, OR BLACK VERNACULAR ENGLISH

Between the exaggerated and nonsensical language of minstrel songs and shows and the language of Zora Neale Hurston's characters in *Their Eyes Were Watching God* is a national debate over the language of black folks. The debate began in the 1970s and resurfaced dynamically in the mid-1990s when the Oakland Public School System in California introduced an initiative to legitimize black vernacular as a necessary teaching strategy for African American children being victimized by the American education system. Relegated to slang and deemed the language of illiterates—and therefore worthless by mainstream educated Americans, both black and white—linguists of African American speech continue to argue that the vernacular language of African Americans is anything but random, syntactically unsophisticated, and indicative of blacks' alleged intellectual inferiority to whites, who set the standards for "proper" and "correct" speech. Zora Neale Hurston's decision to record the language of black folk without apology and annotation connects language with cultural identity, value, and self-empowerment. . . .

The following essay by linguistics professor Karen Adams defines Ebonics and highlights the continuing controversy that connects the language of black people with deeper issues of identity, intellectual capacity, and social worth.

KAREN L. ADAMS, "EBONICS—LANGUAGE OR DIALECT? THE DEBATE CONTINUES" (1998)

A language? A dialect? Slang? Bad English? What is Ebonics? Which answer you get depends on who(m) you ask. For example, when the Oakland school board declared Ebonics a language in 1996, those who consider it slang or uneducated speech that is not appropriate for the classroom were horrified. Some were even surprised by the term Ebonics, combining "ebony" and "phonics," though it had been in use since the 1970s. Others responded that Ebonics is just a dialect of English whose speakers are not in need of the same kind of educational help as Spanish or Vietnamese speaking students. So what is the answer to the question from the viewpoint of a linguist, someone who studies the structure and use of language as a science? Under what category would we be likely to put Ebonics?

Let's start with the difference between a language and a dialect. Linguists are always fond of saying that "a language is a dialect with an army and a navy." We have come to understand that what gets called a "language" or what gets called a "dialect" has nothing much to do with the actual ways that people talk, but with the status of the speakers who are doing the talking. As a matter of fact, to a linguist, a language is a kind of abstraction. Take English, for example. You know that people speak English in a multitude of ways—e.g., British English, Canadian English, Singapore English or American English. And for speakers of American English, there are varieties associated with different regions of the country, with different social groups in these regions, e.g., Valley girl talk, with speakers from different language backgrounds, e.g., Finglish in the North, and so on. No one of these is the English language; it is all of these together, all of its dialects or varieties.

But even as I say this, some of you may be thinking, "Yes, but what about the Queen's English or proper English? That is really the English language." After all, these styles of speaking are certainly different from Ebonics and are declared by teachers and others as "better," and as markers of educated speech. The other forms, such as southern speech, are often referred to as just dialects.

Again, linguists have a different take on this as they think all people learn to speak pretty well. We all grow up speaking like those who nurture us. And whatever the variety our nurturers use, according to the thinking of linguists, this form is "rule-governed." By this we mean that every dialect has rules for pronunciation, rules for the use of grammatical forms, rules for the way we order words in a sentence and rules for making new words. Some rules differ between dialects, but many are shared. And the rules that teachers discuss in the classroom such as the "who" versus "whom" indicated above are a very small set of rules associated most often with writing and learned by most speakers of English only when they start school.

When groups share a speaking style, it is part of what bonds us into a community. Through this speech we are taught, disciplined and loved. But linguists recognize that as some people move into wider and wider communities, they may find quickly that others do not share this speech and may even criticize them for using it. Children learn at a very young age that some ways of speaking are valued over others. Why do some ways become more valued than others? It has very little to do with the different kinds of rules I mentioned above and most to do with the social power and status of the speakers of a variety. For example, the status of southern speech has more to do with the issues leading to the Civil War, the south's defeat and the weak economy of the south after the Civil War than it does with the fact that southern dialects, including in this case Ebonics, do not pronounce the -r- after vowels in words like "car" or "jar." In other parts of the English speaking world, such as Britain, this pronunciation is considered prestigious because the speakers who say this belong to the highest social class.

Those with the greatest wealth traditionally have had the greatest access to education and have also controlled the media. So their pronunciation and the grammatical forms they use become the language of schools and of literacy. People who do not learn these forms as their mother dialect are capable of learning and do learn rule-governed language, but they may not have had equal access to educational resources and to its speakers.

Why so much controversy over Oakland? Some were horrified for many reasons. First, school has been seen as a place where speakers of varieties that are not "high status" can learn the high status variety and hence enter into communities that expect the use of this form. There is no doubt that school language is a kind of variety of wider communication allowing for shared communication norms among many groups. Some were worried that by having Ebonics in the classroom, the opportunity to learn the "standard" or school variety might disappear. Others were upset because they have always been able to use the school variety to set themselves apart and above others, and the Oakland proposal threatened this status and the thinking that their way of speaking is indeed intellectually superior. For those teachers of bilingual classrooms who have struggled to get funds and help for students from second language backgrounds, the prospect of another community tapping into limited resources was difficult.

The Oakland school board, on the other hand, suggested the change because it meant creating a language environment that recognized the role of the nurturer's language in the community and the rule-governed nature of that language. The language of community teaching and the heritage of the community took on value. After all, Ebonics shares language forms and rules that come from African languages. This is the way that many new varieties of languages come about. Speakers of one language learn another and their first language influences their second. This is one of the reasons why English has so much influence from French. Consider the history of the Norman invasion of England in 1066 A.D. These teachers also may know that even linguists do not agree on whether it is harder or easier to learn a second language or a second variety of a language, but they do know from studies in other countries that using one variety, in this case, Ebonics, to teach another variety, e.g., the standard dialect, could work very well.

So is Ebonics a dialect? Yes, but not in any negative sense that some people might argue. Is it a language? Yes, in that languages are just dialects. Is it slang? As it has informal ways of speaking and formal ways of speaking, it may be used informally as an ingroup way of talking just like Valley girl speech is also often considered slang. But it also has the more formal speech of the pulpit and of community leaders. Is it bad? It is never that, though, now, that depends on what you mean by "bad."

PHILIP GOLDSTEIN ON COMPARING *PRIDE AND PREJUDICE* WITH *THEIR EYES WERE WATCHING GOD*

Pride and Prejudice and *Their Eyes* examine the female characters' romantic and marital difficulties, including their gradual division into a public and a private self. In *Pride*, Mrs. Bennet insists that Elizabeth marry Mr. Collins, who will inherit the estate when Mr. Bennet dies. Nanny also tells Janie to marry Logan Killicks in order to gain economic security; however, more serious and practical than Mrs. Bennet,

Nanny claims that Logan's farm will save Janie from the pain, torment, and abandonment which Nanny suffered during and after slavery. Elizabeth considers her mother's insistence ridiculous and with her father's help rejects Mr. Collins's hand, whereas Janie cooperates after Nanny slaps her and pleads with her: "Put me down easy, Janie. Ah'm a cracked plate."[41] Accepting Nanny's fear that romantic love will reduce her to little more than a man's "spit cup," she marries Logan only to discover a limit to or absurdity in Nanny's realism—his toenails are too dirty and his neck too fat for her to love him: "Some folks never was meant to be loved and he's one of them" (22). Nanny defends her realism: "Heah you got uh prop tuh lean on all yo' bawn days, and big protection, and everybody got tuh tip dey hat tuh you and call you Mis' Killicks, and you come worryin' me about love" (22). Janie's complaints kill her ("she dwindled all the rest of the day"[23]) because Nanny's realism cannot exclude Janie's "absurd" belief in love; however, Janie matures: "Janie's first dream was dead, so she became a woman" (24).

Elizabeth's friend Charlotte Lucas faces spinsterhood and economic dependence, rather than a dominating grandmother, but like Janie she marries to gain economic security. To Elizabeth's amazement, the unromantic Charlotte accepts Mr. Collins's offer but, unlike Janie, adroitly adjusts to Collins's absurdities and even to Lady Catherine's officious attentions. Even though Charlotte does not rebel against them, Elizabeth still finds in Charlotte's domestic arrangements and her tactful silences her unstated resistance to them. More importantly, while Elizabeth ridicules and rejects the pompous Mr. Collins and the wealthy Darcy, she, like Charlotte, divides into a public and a private self. For example, Darcy's letter refuting her criticisms of him depresses Elizabeth terribly because she had not expected that his treatment of Wickham or his sister "was capable of a turn which made him entirely blameless throughout the whole."[42] Retiring to her chamber to read the letter or to consult her thoughts, she conceals her private feelings more and more, even from her dear sister Jane. After she decides that he is just the right man for her, she does not admit it publicly, not even when her father ridicules Mr. Collins's warning against her marriage to Darcy. At the end, the novel celebrates their marriage, which unifies their public and private selves; still, as Darcy's influence steadily grows on her, she loses her inclination to laugh at him, and, like Charlotte, develops a meaningful private and an empty public self.

Jody Starks saves Janie from Logan but imposes on Janie a similar but much harsher self-division, as the formal critics say. For instance, he talks with the "big picture" talkers sitting on the porch, but he will not allow her to talk with them. He attends the mule's funeral, delivers an oration, but keeps her at home because he cannot believe that a lady should associate with "such commonness." Most importantly, when she spoils his dinner, he beats her, and, like the town, which keeps its resentment of Jody to itself, she divides into a silent but meaningful private self and a conventional but insignificant public self: "She had an inside and an outside now and suddenly she knew how not to mix them" (68).

Both Hurston and Austen assume that public speech overcomes the division between the characters' public and private selves. For example, Elizabeth often engages in witty public discourse. Unlike Jody Starks, Mr. Bennet grants Elizabeth this (male) privilege, but it embarrasses her mother, who orders her not to "run on in the wild manner that you are suffered to do at home" (29). Elizabeth freely disputes the opinions of one and all, just the same, and thereby wins the ardent admiration of Darcy. After she marries him, she teaches his sister to laugh at him too; still, once she can no longer hate Darcy, she loses her enthusiasm for witty disputation ("It is such a spur to one's genius, such an opening for wit to have a dislike of that kind" [145]).

Austen, who shares the Enlightenment belief that women and men have the same rational faculties, esteems public disputation; by contrast, as Cynthia Bond shows, Hurston considers the porch's "big picture" talk both impotent speech and male domination.[43] At the end Janie has discovered the "impotence" of the public speech, which at the beginning the narrator terms the "mass cruelty" of "the skins" (2); still, to overcome the self-division imposed by Jody, she struggles to engage in public talking. This struggle culminates when, after Joe calls her an old woman, she ridicules his sexual potency: "When you pull down yo' britches, you look lak de change uh life" (75). Jody retreats to his deathbed, sick from a bad liver and a wounded ego. When she tells him that he has never known her true self, he promptly dies—realism precipitates absurdity once again. More importantly, after Jody's death, Janie realizes that she had accepted her grandmother's blind faith in the slave owners' ideals—that owning things counts more than exploring the horizon. Like Sethe, who, as Toni Morrison indicates in *Beloved*, would rather kill her baby than allow Schoolteacher to return it to slavery, she angrily condemns those ideals and, by implication, middle-class realism as well.

Although *Pride* and *Their Eyes* both show that the romantic and marital difficulties faced by the female characters impose on them a self-division alleviated by public speech, *Pride* does not produce such a profound critique of middle-class marriage. Moreover, gradually restricted to Elizabeth's point of view, Austen's third-person narrator demonstrates a limited omniscience which . . . preserves a sharp distinction between standard English and the "vulgar" regional dialects. By contrast, *Their Eyes*, which destroys the opposition of dialect and standard speech, effectively depicts the folk mind of ordinary Blacks, not just the middle classes. In keeping with the Harlem Renaissance, which sought to demonstrate that Black folk culture was not simply the subject of comic minstrelsy but worthy of serious artistic depiction, Hurston, an accomplished anthropologist, cultivated an exceptionally insightful grasp of African-American folk culture.

Notes

41. Zora Neale Hurston, *Their Eyes Were Watching God*, 19. All further citations are from this text.
42. Jane Austen, *Pride and Prejudice*, 133. All further citations are from this text.
43. See Appiah and Gates, *Zora Neale Hurston*, 24–26.

Their Eyes is, almost everyone agrees, a novel about Janie's progressive liberation, her emergence out of objectivity into subjectivity. Her relationship with Tea Cake is the liberating relationship, the one that seems to allow Janie to emerge fully as a subject. But at the same time, this relationship also extends and strengthens the hold of domination over Janie, because Janie no longer even recognizes the domination as domination.[13] . . .

Liberation is always also a form of submission, which is perhaps what leads Joseph Urgo to write, "paradoxically, Hurston equates submission to Tea Cake with Janie's liberation."[15] Thus, though Tea Cake, in one sense, liberates Janie, he also continues a pattern of domination, which becomes evident in his jealousy, his furtive attempts at control, and his physical abuse. This abuse is important because through it Tea Cake firmly asserts his control over Janie, and in this sense, it is a symptom of their relationship. And because this control continues to exist in the relationship with Tea Cake, Janie must kill him; this act—and not her relationship with Tea Cake itself—is the key moment of the novel. It allows Janie to obtain a momentary freedom, to lose her submission to the Other. She becomes, at this moment, a subject separated from the Other, and hence one that bears the weight of a suffocating freedom. Though Tea Cake is a liberatory force in the novel, he also dominates in a new and more pernicious way than either Logan or Joe, and it is this domination that Janie attempts to move beyond when she shoots him. By tracing the path of Janie's subjectivity from the beginning, the necessity of this act will become clear.

Janie's first two marriages—with Logan and Joe—are clearly relationships of domination. The nature of the domination in each case is, however, somewhat different, though they share a fundamental logic. In fact, as Henry Louis Gates has noticed in *The Signifying Monkey*, Janie's first two marriages are thoroughly bourgeois, characterized by a logic of accumulation and possession: "Killicks owns the only organ 'amongst colored folks'; Joe Starks is a man of 'positions and possessions.'"[16] Though both are clearly invested in the prevailing capitalist ideology, we can see in Logan and Joe the contours of two different kinds of capitalism: the ideologies of competitive and monopoly capitalism respectively. The way in which each character dominates Janie indicates the ideological investment of each. Logan demands work out of Janie. He buys a second mule in order to have her work both in the field and in the kitchen: "Ah needs two mules dis yeah. [. . .] Ah aims tuh run two plows, and dis man Ah'm talkin' 'bout is got uh mule all gentled up so even uh woman kin handle 'im" (26). The idea of the work ethic predominates Logan's consciousness and is the driving force in his domination of Janie. It leads him to demand her obedience. He tells her, "You ain't got no particular place. It's wherever Ah need yuh. Git uh move on yuh, and dat quick" (30). The rationale behind such domination lies in the ideology of competitive capitalism—the Protestant work ethic—which, as Jerome Thornton puts it, sees "the role of a woman [as] synonymous to that of a mule."[17]

By forcing Janie into the role of the mule, Logan shatters Janie's imaginary identification: he desecrates the pear tree, Janie's ideal of love and marriage. This alienation, however, marks Janie's birth as subject, her full entry into the symbolic order. Janie first becomes a subject not with her originary dream of the pear tree but, paradoxically, with its "desecration" by Logan Killicks. Janie's relationship with Logan destroys her romantic conception of love: "She knew now that marriage did not make love. Janie's first dream was dead, so she became a woman" (24). Hurston's suggestion here is quite clear, that it is only through loss—of the dream, in this case—not fulfillment, that Janie begins to develop as a subject.[18] Logan dominates Janie and treats her as a "mule" to be commanded, but this domination is necessary for Janie, because it triggers the sense of loss which is constitutive of subject. To become a subject, one must be subjected to the symbolic order in which one's imaginary relation to an object—for Janie, the pear tree—is lost.[19] Without this subjection and loss, there is no subject, because to refuse the loss is to refuse symbolization itself. . . . Janie gains a certain (sexed) identity—"she became a woman"— only when Nanny thrusts her into marriage with Logan and subjects Janie's dream to the exigencies of the Protestant work ethic (which Logan embodies). For Janie, the arrival of Joe Starks indicates her liberation from Logan and the ideological force of this work ethic. After leaving Logan, Janie feels a sense of ecstasy: "What was she losing so much time for? A feeling of newness and change came over her. . . . From now on until death she was going to have flower dust and springtime sprinkled over everything. A bee for her bloom" (31). This is the ecstasy of liberation, but Janie soon learns that she has been liberated into a new kind of domination.

Joe Starks does not dominate Janie by forcing her to labor (as Logan does) but by turning her into a thing, transforming her into his commodity. He doesn't allow her to speak for herself and confines her to the home: "mah wife don't know nothin' 'bout no speech-makin' . . . She's uh woman and her place is in de home" (40–41). Thus, Janie's "liberation," though it releases her from the role of the "mule" into which Logan forced her, becomes, by the same token, an extension of domination, eliminating some of the freedom of movement she enjoyed under Logan. Joe's ideological investment, unlike Logan's, has nothing to do with a work ethic or turning Janie into a "mule"; instead, Joe's stresses control. Through a tightly organized control, Joe dominates Janie in a new way, confining her to a particular position—"her place is in de home"—within a highly organized structure (which he controls). If Logan, with his emphasis on the Protestant work ethic, exhibits the consciousness apropos of competitive capitalism, then Joe exhibits the consciousness apropos of the subsequent epoch— monopoly capitalism. An emphasis on organization—Joe's mode of being-in-the-world—is the primary modification of capitalism effected by monopoly capital; this new model (which supersedes competitive capitalism and "rescues" it) is more efficient than earlier capitalism because it organizes and structures the chaos of competition.[22] . . . Organization is the defining characteristic of monopoly capitalism and its ideology.

While this model liberates its subjects from a devotion to work for work's sake, it also imposes a more complex and diffuse domination—the organization of every sector of society.[25] Janie herself evinces this double aspect of the transition. At first, she feels liberated from Logan and proud to be Joe's wife, but after Joe's organization restricts Janie's behavior, Janie senses that this liberation has an aspect of increased domination to it. As Glynis Carr notes, "Jody demands that [Janie] be not a person but a thing."[26] Hurston describes another feeling of loss in Janie: "It must have been the way Joe spoke out without giving her a chance to say anything one way or another that took the bloom off of things" (41). Joe's need to order everything justifies the severe restrictions he places on Janie's behavior: not allowing her to speak in public, forcing her to keep her hair up, keeping her from the mule's funeral, and not permitting her to join in the "signifying" on the porch of the store. All of these restrictions emanate from Joe's desire to keep Janie in her proper place within his organization.

This predominant aspect of Joe's character is evident not only in his dealings with Janie but in every dimension of his behavior in Eatonville. When he arrives at Eatonville, what irritates Joe most is the disorder. He tells Janie, "God, they call this a town? Why, 'tain't nothing but a raw place in de woods" (32). Joe sees the necessity of organizing the diffuse elements he encounters at "Eatonville" (even the name is not yet "organized"—"Some say West Maitland and some say Eatonville" [34]). . . . In "Eatonville," . . . there are diffuse elements which Joe organizes, just as the monopoly does, around a coherent center (himself). This is not to say that Joe *represents* monopoly capitalism (any more than Logan represents competitive or liberal capitalism), but that his subjectivity is structured by its logic. It is thus not surprising that Joe's first actions involve an attempt to effect a centered organization. He tells the people of Eatonville that "everything is got tuh have uh center and uh heart to it, and uh town ain't no different from nowhere else" (38). In this way, Joe justifies building his store as the town meeting place and insisting that the town have a mayor (which, not coincidentally, turns out to be him). Through the character of Joe, Hurston presents the ideological form of domination endemic to monopoly capitalism: a totalized whole organized around a legitimating and controlling center.

Hurston's novel shows clearly that Joe, while he does provide liberation of a sort from the domination of Logan, further confines Janie and creates a new kind of domination. The other characters in the novel feel this domination as well:

> There was something about Joe Starks that cowed the town. It was not because of physical fear. He was no fist fighter. His bulk was not even imposing as men go. Neither was it because he was more literate than the rest. Something else made men give way before him. He had a bow-down command in his face, and every step he took made the thing more tangible. (44)

There is something tautological about the phenomenon Hurston describes here; according to this description, Joe becomes an authority in Eatonville because . . . he is an authority. That is, the people in the town obey Joe for only one reason: he acts as if he is to be obeyed. Joe's power does not come from a tangible quality—strength, intelligence, and so on—but from the appearance of authority and a corresponding willingness to obey, to bow before authority, among the people of Eatonville. Hurston describes the dynamics of Joe's authority further: "The town had a basketful of feelings good and bad about Joe's positions and possessions, but none had the temerity to challenge him. They bowed down to him rather, because he was all of these things, and then again he was all of these things because the town bowed down" (47). Joe's authority, his power over the town and over Janie, does not exist in itself, it exists only insofar as they invest him with this authority, insofar as they recognize his authority.[28] . . .

Like Joe, Tea Cake appears, in the first instance, to be a purely liberating force in Janie's life. Jerome E. Thornton sees a "unity" in their relationship, which "is symbolized by the way in which Janie both shares in the fun times of her man and community and works along side Tea Cake in the bean fields."[35] It is clear, from Tea Cake's treatment of Janie, that he is not Joe Starks. But perhaps Tea Cake, again like Joe, appears liberatory at first and then, in a way Janie (and maybe even Hurston herself) is not conscious of, actually inaugurates a new kind of domination, significantly different from the organized domination of Joe Starks.

Tea Cake's domination, if that is what it is, certainly differs in appearance from Joe's. In fact, it seems at first as if Tea Cake represents pure liberation from the organized structure of Joe's domination without then imposing his own form on Janie. Janie directly opposes Tea Cake to various capitalist forms of domination. Janie tells Pheoby that "Tea Cake ain't no Jody Starks" and that their relationship "ain't no *business proposition*, and no race after *property* and *titles*. Dis is uh love game. Ah done lived Grandma's way, now I means tuh live mine" (108, my emphasis). In contrast to Joe's constant emphasis on using Janie to establish his own importance and on keeping Janie in a preestablished place, Tea Cake liberates Janie from the confines of a tightly organized economy. This is evident not only when Tea Cake invites Janie to play checkers, but also, perhaps most clearly, in the move he proposes to her. Whereas Joe takes Janie from the country—the periphery—into (what would become) the organized structure of a city—the center—Tea Cake takes her from the city to the "muck." In describing the muck to Janie, Tea Cake tells her, "Folks don't do nothin' down dere but make money and fun and foolishness. We must go dere" (122). Hurston is clear about the effect on Janie: "He drifted off to sleep and Janie looked down on him and felt a self-crushing love. So her soul crawled out from its hiding place" (122). The prospect of "fun and foolishness," a prospect which Tea Cake will help her to realize, liberates Janie from the tyranny of Joe's restrictive organizational structure, and this liberation indicates a new epoch in her life.

In this liberation, however, just as in Joe's liberation, there is also a reverse side, a side of domination. This domination appears most explicitly in Tea Cake's jealousy and subsequent abuse of Janie. Hurston notes,

> When Mrs. Turner's brother came and she brought him over to be introduced, Tea Cake had a brainstorm. Before the week was over he had whipped Janie. Not because her behavior justified his jealousy, but it relieved that awful fear inside him. Being able to whip her reassured him in possession. No brutal beating at all. He just slapped her around a bit to show he was boss. (140)

Just like Joe Starks, Tea Cake must be certain of his relation of domination vis-à-vis Janie, that he is "boss." He whips Janie to demonstrate this domination to Mrs. Turner: "Ah jus' let her see dat Ah got control" (141). Although Tea Cake dominates in a new way, he does continue to dominate. Tea Cake's transformation after he contracts rabies, viewed in the aftermath of his earlier jealous rage, becomes symptomatic rather than anomalous. As Thomas Cassidy points out, "Tea Cake's transformation after the dog bite does not seem to be the result of a totally foreign element invading his psyche as much as an acceleration of forces already evident in his personality before the storm. The jealous violence of the mad Tea Cake is prefigured by the jealous violence of the Tea Cake who slaps Janie around."[36] In other words, after the dog bite, Tea Cake becomes *explicitly* what he already was *implicitly*. The bite of the rabid dog is not the cause of this transformation—as the common sense interpretation would have it—but the completely contingent moment that provided the opportunity for Tea Cake to become what he already was.[37] Cassidy rightly claims that "Tea Cake's character change after the storm is little more than an intensification of the growing jealousy which he had been feeling before the storm."[38] This growing jealousy— and its ultimate threat of lethal violence toward Janie—suggests that Tea Cake, while certainly a liberating figure in one sense, also brings to Janie a new kind of domination, which is one with his mode of liberation.[39] . . .

Tea Cake does not pursue Janie because he hopes to possess her fortune, but when he discovers her hidden two-hundred dollars, he spends it all on a party, because "he was excited and felt like letting folks know who he was" (117). Though Tea

Cake has no designs on stealing Janie's fortune, when he sees her hidden money, he takes it "out of curiosity," and after he takes it, his only thoughts are his own "immediate gratification" and the image he can project of himself, rather than a concern for what Janie might think about his (and the money's) absence. In this way, Tea Cake both acts out the role of the pathological narcissist and molds Janie into that role. Thus, Tea Cake dominates Janie not merely through control or violence but through the new imperative he brings to her: Enjoy![41]

Though Tea Cake wins the money back through gambling, this incident furthers Janie's dependence on him by exacerbating the self-doubt that she already feels.[42] Doubt has plagued Janie from the beginning of her relationship with Tea Cake; after their first night together Tea Cake leaves for work and doesn't return, sparking doubt in Janie:

> In the cool of the afternoon the fiend from hell specially sent to lovers arrived at Janie's ear. Doubt. All the fears that circumstance could provide and the heart feel, attacked her on every side. If only Tea Cake would make her certain! He did not return that night nor the next and so she plunged into the abyss and descended to the ninth darkness where light has never been. (103)

Similarly, after Tea Cake takes the money and throws a party, doubt overcomes Janie, who begins to compare herself to Annie Tyler, another wealthy widow who lost all of her money to an opportunistic young lover. Though in both cases Tea Cake returns and professes his uninterrupted love for Janie, the effect of these absences—and the doubt they engender—is to make Janie all the more devoted to Tea Cake and more susceptible to his control. . . .

Even at the height of their love, Janie has gnawing suspicions about Tea Cake's fidelity, seeing him stray away with Nunkie (130–131). Furthermore, Janie remains wholly dependent on Tea Cake and their love relation, despite the way in which their love has elevated her ego. Rather than freeing Janie from domination, her love for Tea Cake moves domination to a new level—one at which Janie herself is invested in that which dominates her.

Notes

13. Joseph Urgo correctly sees that domination exists in each of Janie's relationships: "The mistake easily made in reading the novel as a progression from bad to mediocre to best mate for Janie is to miss the repetition of treatment Janie receives from each man. Each man seeks domination, each man seeks possession. Each man physically assaults her" (Joseph Urgo, "'The Tune Is the Unity of the Thing': Power and Vulnerability in Zora Neale Hurston's *Their Eyes Were Watching God*," *Southern Literary Journal* 23 [1991]: 52). What Urgo's otherwise insightful point misses is that not only does each successive man in Janie's life continue to dominate her, but that each also expands this domination, precisely because it comes to seem less and less like domination (both to Janie and to many readers of the novel).

15. Urgo, "Tune Is the Unity," 52.

16. Gates, *Signifying Monkey*, 186.

17. Jerome Thornton, "'Goin' on de Muck': The Paradoxical Journey of the Black American Hero," *CLA Journal* 31 (1988): 264. In *The Protestant Ethic and the Spirit of Capitalism*, Max Weber identifies (what was originally) Christian asceticism with the spirit of capitalism. According to such asceticism, "not leisure and enjoyment, but only activity serves to increase the glory of God, according to the definite manifestations of His will" (Max Weber, *The Protestant Ethic and the Spirit of Capitalism*, trans. Talcott Parsons [London: Routledge, 1992], 157). The ideology of asceticism has as its archetype the hard-working individual—Logan Killicks. What Weber does not discuss—and what is revealed in Hurston's novel—are the subsequent "spirit(s) of capitalism" which follow in the wake of asceticism.

18. It is Hegel who first conceived of the necessity of an initial loss for the dialectic of the subject to commence. For his well-known discussion of this aspect of Hegel's thought, see Alexandre Kojève, *Introduction to the Reading of Hegel: Lectures on the "Phenomenology of Spirit,"* trans. James H. Nichols Jr. [Ithaca, NY: Cornell University Press, 1969].

19. Lacan defines the symbolic order as the world where objects are lost, where we get the symbol in place of the object.

22. The transition from liberal to monopoly capitalism, as Paul Baran and Paul Sweezy note in their *Monopoly Capital*, effects "a shift in the center of gravity from production to sales" (Paul A. Baran and Paul M. Sweezy, *Monopoly Capital: An Essay on the American Economic and Social Order* [New York: Monthly Review Press, 1966], 131). This shift is directly homologous to the change in emphasis from

work ethic to organization—and from Logan to Joe. Whereas Logan is only concerned with his own (and Janie's) production, Joe must concern himself with marketing both himself and Janie to others. This is why, though Janie is not forced to work, she must occupy a certain symbolic position, above the interaction of the other citizens of Eatonville.

25. Because monopoly capitalism is oriented ideologically around organization, the mode of subjectivity which corresponds to it is not the "autonomous" individual devoted to the work ethic, but the "organization man," devoted to being accepted and loved by the group—following its rules—rather than differentiating him/herself.

26. Glynis Carr, "Storytelling as *Bildung* in Zora Neale Hurston's *Their Eyes Were Watching God*," *CLA Journal* 31 (1987): 197.

28. One can see the parallel here between Joe's authority and that of Delamere in *The Marrow of Tradition;* both lack any substantial ground and are purely the product of belief.

35. Thornton, "'Goin' on de Muck,'" 267.

36. Thomas Cassidy, "Janie's Rage: The Dog and the Storm in *Their Eyes Were Watching God*," *CLA Journal* 36 (1993): 264.

37. The rabid dog's bite is a moment of transition, in Hegel's terms, from self to for-itself. At this point, Tea Cake's domination of Janie, which has been unconscious, comes to consciousness. If we recognize this continuity in Tea Cake's domination of Janie, it becomes clear Tea Cake's physical abuse is not something exceptional, but symptomatic. This is what John Lowe misses when he laments recent critical attacks on Tea Cake and accuses Tea Cake's detractors of "presentism." Lowe claims, "Readings that insist on applying contemporary standards to texts written in and about a different culture almost sixty years in the past are simply ahistorical presentist interpretations of both literature and culture. It is worth noting that until this line of argument was raised, many critics quite rightly praised this novel as one of the great love stories in our literature; unfortunately, that reading seems to be receding as an important but not definitive detail of the narrative has been interpreted out of context" (Lowe, *Jump at the Sun*, 187). In other words, without this "important but not definitive detail," there would be no ground for seeing domination on the part of Tea Cake. What this argument fails to see is that this domination is far from being limited to this one incident, but pervades the entirety of Tea Cake and Janie's relationship. In fact, the physical abuse is not even one of the more significant indications of Tea Cake's control over Janie, because it is a moment where his ideological authority breaks down and, as he is forced to exercise his power, his weakness is exposed.

38. Cassidy, "Janie's Rage," 264.

39. For a discussion of Tea Cake's domination of Janie throughout their relationship, see Carla Kaplan, "The Erotics of Talk: 'That

Oldest Human Longing' in *Their Eyes Were Watching God*," *American Literature* 67 (1995): 115–142. Kaplan's excellent essay also counters attempts to see *Their Eyes* as a celebration of voice and community. She argues that "the reconciliation of Janie and her community argued for by contemporary critics derives, I think, from our own nostalgia and longing for forms of communal life" (Kaplan, "Erotics," 135).

41. In *The Metastases of Enjoyment*, Žižek points out that this command "Enjoy!" is the precise way in which domination works today: "In post-liberal societies, [. . .] the agency of social repression no longer acts in the guise of an internalized Law or Prohibition that requires renunciation and self-control; instead, it assumes the form of a hypnotic agency that imposes the attitude of 'yielding to temptation'—that is to say, its injunction amounts to a command: 'Enjoy yourself!'" (Slavoj Žižek, *The Metastases of Enjoyment: Six Essays on Woman and Causality* [New York: Verso, 1994], 16).

42. The fact that Tea Cake restores Janie's money through gambling is not an insignificant detail, but one that confirms his mode of subjectivity as that of the pathological narcissist. Unlike Logan Killicks, the devotee of the work ethic, Tea Cake stakes his fundamental belief in chance rather than in work. That the game is dice offers further indication of this. As David Sheppard notes, "Not cards—there would be some skill involved in that—but dice, a game of pure chance" (David Sheppard, "Living by Comparisons: Janie and Her Discontents," *English Language Notes* 30 [1992]: 71).

PAMELA GLENN MENKE ON VOODOO ELEMENTS IN THE NOVEL

When twenty-five-year-old Zora Neale Hurston "headed her toenails" to New Orleans in 1928, she began the mystical journey that would take her from New Orleans, to the Bahamas, Jamaica, and Haiti—a journey that would deeply influence her fiction (*Mules* 183). Although Hurston became familiar with conjuring and root work during her growing-up years in Florida, the catalyst for what John Lowe has described as Hurston's "cosmic" consciousness was her four-month sojourn in New Orleans (334). There, she literally acquired what Moses obtains from the Ethiopian Jethro in Hurston's Biblical revision, *Moses, Man of the Mountain* (1939), "the black cat bone and snake wisdom" (280). She became deeply engaged in the voodoo worship, mystery, and ritual that would provide her mystical home, her site of legendary being, her place of creative power, and the source of an imagistic vocabulary to refigure her world. As Karla Holloway insists, Hurston's "vodu" study opened for her the "potential of the black word to 'know the thunder' and 'summon gods'" (111). Gained at great personal risk through disciplined preparation, ritual, sacrifice, and reverence, voodoo served as more than a metaphor for Hurston. It served as a dark and powerful alternative to the rigidity, hypocrisy and formality of a white-inscribed Eurocentric worldview. . . .

Hurston wrote *Their Eyes* during her Haitian immersion in a sacred realm filled with astonishing mysteries far surpassing New Orleans hoodoo and Jamaican obeah. She describes her compulsion to produce the novel: "It was damned up in me, and I wrote it under internal pressure in seven weeks" (*Tracks* 212). Hemenway remarks that "Haiti released a flood of language and emotion," but attributes a large part of the emotion to a passionate, "stormy," and "doomed" love affair between Hurston and a West Indian, a response that Hurston herself prompts in *Dust Tracks* (Hemenway 230–31). Nellie McKay, who also notes the autobiographical elements, views the novel as emancipatory, the "forging a new history constructed out of the handing down of one woman's story of liberation to another" as does Susan Willis, who offers Pheoby's decision to make Sam take her fishing as "the book's radical single statement" that reconstitutes "domestic life and space" (McKay 68; Willis 52, 159). Other critics also note the direct Haitian connection,[4] but they focus on the rich complexity of the vernacular, authorial, and communal voices in *Their Eyes* and on the Afrocentric expressions central to Hurston's narrative strategies. Baker and Holloway position their interpretations within the "image work" of conjure and Afrocentric word, but they do not pursue the intertextual resonances with Hurston's hoodoo/voodoo allegiance and knowledge (Baker 63). For example, Pheoby gains the ability from "Janie's revealed images . . . to both read and write the world in new and liberating ways" as Baker suggests; however, Pheoby is at a remarkably vulnerable and early stage of her imagistic journey (Baker 63). She may not be in Janie's "still bait" (138) stage, but she is nowhere close to approaching Janie's mystic power. While Pheoby will insist Sam take her fishing, Janie is gathering the entire mystic world in her "fish-net" (184). Hurston enacts her fictional counterpart Janie as a legendary figure within in a site generated by Afrocentric legend, myth, and ritual; in the process, Hurston creates a lingual Mambo based on her Louisiana and Haitian hoodoo/voodoo initiations and her serious participation in conjuring. *Their Eyes* and *Tell My Horse* reveal and confirm Hurston's spiritual, creative, and anthropological truth: the agents of vision are the people themselves; the spirit dreams and demons are those they themselves mouth. As she states in the one-sentence introduction to the chapter that gives *Tell My Horse* its title, "Gods always behave like the people who make them" (219). *Their Eyes* becomes for Hurston a purging of male-dominant voodoo and an expression of her own sacredness, a making of her own Mambo. She creates a central female figure who first accepts and then releases the communal God, who engages in rituals of blood sacrifice. She then awards her the gift of tongue and the ability to conjure. . . .

Two separate, seemingly unconnected images of stones and mud-balls from *Tell My Horse* and *Their Eyes* place the legendary Shango, whose name Hurston carries in *Mules and Men*, at the center of her creative spirit. In Haiti, as she was completing *Their Eyes*, Hurston visited the Isle De La Gonave, a womanly place of special peace: "I found on this remote island a peace I have never known anywhere else on earth. La Gonave is the mother of peace. Its outlines which from Port-au-Prince look like a sleeping woman, are prophetic" (135). Hurston then repeats a Haitian legend about a sleeping goddess who has in her grasp the god's message of peace: "When she wakes up, she will give it to the people" (134). On this island, Hurston learns about the "loa-" or spirit-invested stones. Some are stone implements of "gone aborigines," and others are stones of a particular shape and color, but all are filled with the presence of Shango, "who hurls his bolts and makes stones that are full of power" (*Horse* 136). Explains Hurston, these stones, inhabited by and emblematic of gods and legendary ancestors, are ritually baptized, placed on family altars, and handed down from generation to generation.

In *Their Eyes*, we again encounter the godly stones as Hurston transforms her imaged La Gonave sleeping woman into the awakening Janie. The mystical power of the magic stones has been submerged in the deadening "muck" of everyday existence, and Janie has become "still-bait" (138). Jealous angels have battered, fragmented, and beaten the God-made glittering humans; nothing is left but a "little spark" with a "shine and a song." Still dissatisfied, the angels have encased each little spark in mud; the lonesome spark persists, but the "mud is deaf and dumb" (139). In her grandmother's and Joe's outside worlds, Janie is "still-bait," a passive creature awaiting consumption (138). In her inside world, however, Janie has the magic stone power of shine. Chipping away the deaf and dumb mud of her obeisance to others, she is a "mud-ball" whose shine is beginning to glimmer. At the conclusion of the novel, she has contradicted her grandmother, Killicks, Joe, and Tea Cake and their destructive definitions of reality; she is at one with her dream vision. As Janie goes to her sacred bedroom, she carries a light "like a spark of sunstuff" (139, 285). Janie's ability to discover, to make, and to be part of sacred meaning lights her way. She has the gift of creation, and the stuff of that creation lies within her memory. She fashions and embraces the living essence of Tea Cake. . . .

Janie's historical self is enmeshed in a God image that requires blood sacrifice. To be coupled with a man requires worshiping his God-given dominance. She is "possessed" by him and by the male images of God; she must dispossess her "self" to secure her historical and spiritual freedom. The sacrificial rituals Janie performs to end this "possession" use the weapons of her victims. She first achieves her victims' "dreams" and then cuts them away in the quest for her own.

Janie first destroys the hope of her grandmother Nanny, who stands as the damaged "foundation of ancient power that no longer mattered" (26). Nanny, who lives through sacrifice, believes in the Christian Lord's provisions: "De Lawd will provide." Her dream is one of male protection; her fears are of male supremacy. "De white man throw down de load and tell de nigger man tuh pick it up. He pick it up because he have to, but he don't tote it. He hand it to his womenfolks. . . . Ah been prayin' fuh it tuh be different wid you" (29). Janie's marriage to Logan Killicks seems to fulfill Nanny's dream: "you is wid de onliest organ in town, amongst colored folks, in yo' parlor. Got a house bought and paid for and sixty acres uh land" (41). Janie's subsequent disgust for Logan Killicks not only shatters Nanny's dream of a proud married life, it also destroys Nanny. Dismayed by Janie's continuing vision of romantic love, Nanny dies a broken woman.

Janie then sacrifices Joe Starks and Tea Cake. Joe with his repetitive exclamation "I God" teaches her the killing power of words. Henry Louis Gates identifies Joe's authorial power as "the figure of the male author . . . who has authored both Eatonville and Janie's existences" (206). Joe has a dream of his own self-construction: "Ah told you in de very first beginnin' dat Ah aimed tuh be uh big voice. You oughta be glad, 'cause dat makes uh big woman outa you" (74). Imprisoned by his male behavior, Janie learns to pretend and to mix her "inside thing and her outside thing" (113): "Maybe he ain't nothin', but he is something in my mouth. He's got tuh be else Ah ain't got nothin' tuh live for. Ah'll lie and say he is" (118). Increasingly disillusioned, she begins to challenge his supremacy. When he makes bitter fun of her sagging "rump," she spits him out of her mouth: "Talkin' 'bout me lookin' old! When you pull down yo' britches, you look lak de change uh life" (123). She rids herself of the lie and, figuratively, of him. According to her friend Pheoby, the power of Janie's words is believed by some to be the result of conjuring, "a fix" (127). Distraught with Pheoby's information about the town rumors, Janie goes to the ailing Joe and confronts him: "Mah own mind had tuh be squeezed and crowded out tuh make room for yours in me" (133). She literally talks him into impotence and death: "Janie had robbed him of his illusion of irresistible maleness. . . . There was nothing to do in life anymore" (123–24).

Janie's final sacrifice is Tea Cake. Janie confesses to Tea Cake her fearful reluctance to trust him: "Oh, Tea Cake, don't make no false pretense wid me!" He promises vigorously, "Janie, Ah hope God may kill me, if Ah'm lyin'" (165). Ironically and appropriately, God does just that. Tea Cake dallies with Nunkie and then, like his charismatic fictional predecessor preacher John, "whips" Janie for standing up to him. And two gods get him. The destructive hurricane God produces the mad dog whose bite robs Tea Cake of sense and self. Next the human Janie literally kills him and then consumes her sweet Tea Cake, awarding him eternal life in her truth dreams.

Tea Cake, like Nanny, is fooled by a God who betrays him. Good times and laughter serve as Tea Cake's god. A perpetual gambler, Tea Cake, grinning and shooting dice, discounts the hurricane. Janie hears the rolling thunder that heralds the destructive God enslaving them all: "Ole Massa is doin' His work now" (235). Bitten by the mad dog, Tea Cake becomes a jealous "fiend" who takes a pistol and aims it at Janie. Tea Cake's bullet misses Janie, but her sure shot destroys him. In that death-giving act, Janie proclaims her own transformation. As the narrator explains, Janie is no longer "her sacrificing self" (273). Tea Cake's claiming of Janie is ended. Blood sacrifice completed, Janie's historical self is eradicated. The male God of possession and the woman's companion dream of self-sacrifice are concluded.

Notes
4. Significantly, Henry Louis Gates, Jr., Gayl Jones, Michael Awkward, and John Callahan.

DIANA MILES ON FEMALE IDENTITY AND REBIRTH

By reading *Their Eyes Were Watching God* as an ethically driven testimony to personal and historical trauma, we can begin to fully understand the impetus behind Hurston's desire to radically disrupt those social orders that sought to entrap women in a variety of ways. In 1937, Hurston wrote *Their Eyes* in seven weeks while on a Guggenheim fellowship in Haiti to research Obeah practices in the West Indies.[9] The novel presents an unusual figure in American letters—a poor, black, rural, questing woman whom Hurston calls Janie Crawford. While much of the novel is set in a small Florida town that recalls Hurston's own Eatonville, Janie travels, marries, gains wisdom, and returns to pass it on.

Because the novel is told retrospectively, Janie's narrative begins as she returns home. Her actual quest begins as her pubescent sexuality emerges. Janie defines sexual communion through the natural process of reproduction—specifically through the image of a "pear tree soaking in the alto chant of visiting bees" (11). In contrast to this image, Nanny, Janie's grandmother, forces her into a marriage with Logan Killicks, an old man with a home and sixty acres. When the marriage falls short of her vision, Janie runs off with Jody Starks, who brings her to an all-black Florida town (16). As mayor of the town, Jody's words become law while Janie is virtually silenced. After Jody's death, Janie marries a younger man, Tea Cake, and her journey continues as they travel together to the South Florida Everglades, or the "Muck." There, Janie finds her own voice, and he teaches her important lessons about survival, including how to shoot a gun. After accidentally becoming infected with rabies, Tea Cake turns on Janie, and in order to save herself, she shoots him. Their relationship reflects both Janie's joy at having found her pear-tree love and the sorrow of his death. The narration takes place in the intimate setting of Janie's porch. As Janie gives her story over to her "kissin' friend" Pheoby, a transformation occurs that causes Pheoby to "'[grow] ten feet higher from jus' listenin'" (7, 192).

As Pheoby's transformation demonstrates, *Their Eyes* is a compelling tale driven by Hurston's demand for altered conceptions of women's identities. The questing heroine was, during Hurston's lifetime, a radical figure. Not only does Hurston's heroine leave an oppressive yet secure community in search of selfhood, but she honors the ethical demand to give testimony to other women, encouraging them to first define and then satisfy their own passions. *Their Eyes* demonstrates Hurston's personal commitment to this demand, which stems from the fact that the text also seeks to portray her own inner self. As Elizabeth Fox-Genovese notes, *Their Eyes* "offers Hurston's most sustained attempt to provide some representations of her own emotional life."[10] Hurston fashions herself in the character of Janie as a way of giving testimony to the violence and oppression she encountered in intimate relationships between men and women. This novel also adds her testimony to that of other women, particularly her mother and grandmother, whose lives she examines through the characters of Lucy Potts and Amy Crittenden in her first novel, *Jonah's Gourd Vine* (1934).

Janie's ability to exude independence and wisdom depends on an understanding of the women in *Jonah's Gourd Vine*, which situates Hurston's perspective on womanhood relative to her own family history. Her capacity for independence and wisdom are legacies from Amy Crittenden, Lucy Potts, and the other women of Notasulga, Alabama.[11] Through the female characters in *Jonah's Gourd Vine*, Hurston begins the historical and psychological development of the acclaimed model of female liberation found in the character of Janie Crawford. Through *Their Eyes*, Hurston defines herself as a woman in relation to the legacy of women who went before her and, most significantly, to those who, she imagined, would go after her.

These interlocking relationships between generations of women underscore the importance of establishing an audience of secondary witnesses when giving testimony. According to Laub, secondary witnesses are essential to documenting and thereby preventing the trauma from recurring: "For the testimonial process to take place, there needs to be a bonding, the intimate and total presence of an *other*—in the position of one who hears. Testimonies are not monologues; they cannot take place in solitude."[12] By writing fiction, Hurston establishes a body of witnesses to receive her own personal testimony.

The significant correspondences between Hurston's life and the character of Janie suggests that *Their Eyes* is organized around an ethical imperative to give testimony to the traumas that Hurston both witnessed and experienced. One of the most striking correspondences is the similarity between the true-love relationship between Janie and Tea Cake and the older woman–younger man relationship Hurston had had with a man she only identifies as A.W.P. They first met in New York in 1931. He was a twenty-three-year-old college student and she a forty-year-old writer, anthropologist, and folklorist. In her autobiography, *Dust Tracks on a Road* (1942), Hurston describes his domination of her and the violence of their relationship. She explains that he was

> the master kind. All, or nothing, for him. The terrible thing was that neither could leave each other alone. . . . Let me seem too cordial with any male and something was going to happen. Just let him smile too broad at any woman, and no sooner did we get inside my door than the war was on! One night . . . I slapped his face. That was a mistake. He was still smoldering from an incident a week old. A fellow had just met us on Seventh Avenue and kissed me on my cheek. Just one of those casual things, but it had burned up A.W.P. So I had unknowingly given him an opening he had been praying for. He paid me off then and there with interest. No broken bones, you understand, and no black eyes. . . . Then I knew I was too deeply in love to be my old self. For always a blow to my body had infuriated me beyond measure. . . . But somehow I didn't hate him at all. . . . (186, 187)

Hurston goes on to say that when she wrote *Their Eyes*, she was getting over this affair and "tried to embalm all the tenderness of [her] passion for him" in the novel (*Dust Tracks* 188, 189). Her use of the word "embalm" is a telling choice for describing the end of a violent relationship; the relevance of her word choice becomes apparent in the fictional scene where Janie and Tea Cake's affair ends because she shoots him as he is about to attack her. Hurston also gives testimony to the violence of her relationship with A.W.P. through a beating that Janie receives from Tea Cake so that he can publicly assert ownership of her. In the same way that A.W.P. beat Hurston because another man may have shown some affection for her, Tea Cake explains that he "'didn't whop Janie 'cause *she* done

nothin'. [He] beat her tuh show dem Turners who is boss'"
(141). Further correspondence between Janie and Tea Cake's
affair and Hurston and A.W.P.'s relationship appears in the
post-beating intimacy between Janie and Tea Cake. Just as Tea
Cake is described as having "petted and pampered [Janie] as
if those two or three face slaps had nearly killed her" (140). In
her autobiography, Hurston says that after A.W.P. beat her,
they "were more affectionate than ever" (*Dust Tracks* 187).[13]
Ultimately, *Their Eyes* reflects upon Hurston's own vulnerability
to male domination. The text serves as a venue for testimony
and affords her a place where she can design an ideal self in the
form of the character Janie who speaks to other women about
self-love and independence. . . .

In *Their Eyes*, the only detailed discussion of sexual
reproduction comes from Janie's grandmother, Nanny. Nanny's
motherhood is the direct result of her master's coercion, while
Janie is the product of her mother's rape (17, 19); hence, both
Janie and her mother result from violently enforced heterosexual
encounters. Perhaps for this reason, Hurston renders a heroine
whose three marriages, which also hold varied levels of violence,
produce no biological children. Unlike her grandmother or her
mother, Janie's generation of women has a wider range of life
choices. She is neither a slave woman nor a second-generation
slave woman. Janie's life in an all-black town, mobility, and
cultural literacy expand her horizons. While Hurston's heroine
inherits the legacy of intergenerational trauma from Nanny
and her mother, she does not fully repeat the entrapment of
patriarchal domination by producing biological children with
men who claim ownership over her body. Through Janie,
Hurston renders a liberated female who reproduces descendants
outside the boundaries of patriarchy.

The violence associated with Janie's three marriages has
impregnated her with the seed of alterity that implicitly rejects
reproduction of and with males in favor of self-reproduction.
The psychic split that impairs Janie's speech in the courtroom
signals the birth of another self—a consciousness articulated by
the desire to testify to the experience of violent and oppressive
heterosexual relationships. When Janie returns home, it is

Pheoby, her "kissin'-friend," who correctly identifies as a descendant the woman that Janie's experiences produced: "[Y]ou sho looks *good*. You looks like youse yo' own daughter. . . . Even wid dem overhalls on, you shows yo' womanhood" (4).

Heterosexual relationships often produce children who, on a variety of levels, bind the man, the woman, and their history together. In contrast, Hurston renders the violence of Janie's heterosexual relationships as producing a split in consciousness that facilitates an alternate form of reproduction. Janie births her own daughter; this daughter-descendent is her speaking self. *Their Eyes Were Watching God* employs

> a "narrative strategy of the multiple individual," . . . her power is articulated in and continued through a community that is formed in direct answer to the claims of love and romance. Not only is the traditional heterosexual couple supplanted as emphasis of the action, but it is replaced by interchangeable versions of the same-sex couple: mother and daughter, sisters, lovers, narrator and audience. . . . Perhaps most significantly, the mother–daughter relation is continuously transformed.[45]

Hurston not only transforms the mother–daughter relationship, but she goes much further by expanding the boundaries of female reproduction. Her depiction of Janie suggests that a traumatic split of consciousness can, eventually, function as a reproductive source for a new and powerful identity, which is shared with other females in the community.

> The collaborative model of maternal influence suggests a subversively extended family romance, in which the mother as co-creator is simultaneously parent of the writer and her lover or spouse. Most disruptively, for the absolute status of all these role definitions, she may even become the daughter of her own daughter.[46]

Hurston's self-reflection, Janie, models women's ability to give birth to the next generation of women without heterosexual love—without having to grant male access to, or power over, their bodies. In fact, the emergent speaking woman who "looks like [Janie's] own daughter," has full control of her own text only after she has murdered Tea Cake—her rabidly jealous lover. Her ability to rebirth herself as her own daughter is contingent upon her ability to love herself more than she loves him.[47] The self-articulated claim to her own voice is prefigured by her ability to kill off a violent and rabid love affair.

As *Their Eyes Were Watching God* demonstrates, in order for women to heal psychologically from the trauma of patriarchal domination, they must produce bodies of testimony. Hurston's desire to promote social changes stems from her own personal experiences. The impact of her traumatic experiences dictates the direction of her work and reveals that Hurston was often "caught in the dilemma of how she might both govern and exploit the autobiographical impulses that partially direct her [texts]."[48] *Their Eyes Were Watching God*, and her first novel, *Jonah's Gourd Vine*, establish an important historical, cultural, and experiential line of kinship for black female novelists writing later in the twentieth century. Ultimately, these texts become maternal sites that allow an autonomous form of reproduction that instigates the disruption of social orders.

Notes

9. Obeah or "magic," as practiced in Haiti, forms part of the Haitian polytheistic Voodoo religion. In an effort to trace the diasporic presence of African religious systems, Hurston set out to compare the religious practices in Jamaica and Haiti with what she found still in use among African Americans. For further reading see Hurston's *Tell My Horse: Voodoo and Life in Haiti and Jamaica* (New York: Perennial Library, 1990).

10. Elizabeth Fox-Genovese, "My Statue, My Self. Autobiographical Writings of Afro-American Women," *Reading Black, Reading Feminist*, ed. Henry Louis Gates (New York: Penguin, 1990) 195.

11. The town of Notasulga, Alabama, is both the setting of *Jonah's Gourd Vine* and Hurston's actual birthplace. Both her parents and grandparents originate there. Chapters 1 and 2 establish the relationship between Hurston's personal testimony in *Their Eyes* and the lives of her foremothers.

12. Dori Laub, "Bearing Witness or the Vicissitudes of Listening," *Testimony: Crisis of Witnessing in Literature, Psychoanalysis, and History*,

Shoshana Felman and Dori Laub (New York: Routledge, 1992) 70–71.

13. In *Jonah's Gourd Vine*, Hurston describes a similar intimacy between the fictional personas of her parents, John and Lucy Potts. See chapter 2 for a discussion of the intimate bedroom scene, which immediately follows John's use of a loaded Winchester rifle to threaten Lucy if she ever tries to leave him (111).

45. Molly Hite, "Romance, Marginality, and Matrilineage: *The Color Purple* and *Their Eyes Were Watching God*," 447.

46. Molly Hite, "Romance, Marginality, and Matrilineage: *The Color Purple* and *Their Eyes Were Watching God*," 449.

47. In her first novel, *Jonah's Gourd Vine*, the persona of Hurston's mother, Lucy Pearson, speaks to her daughter from her deathbed; she says, "'don' love anybody better'n you do yo'self. Do, you'll be dying befo' yo time is out . . . uh person can he killed 'thout being struck uh blow'" (130).

48. Robert Stepto, *From Behind the Veil: A Study of Afro-American Narrative* (Urbana: U of Illinois P, 1979) 166.

SHAWN E. MILLER ON CONFLICTING READINGS OF THE NOVEL'S CONCLUSION

Of course, the book does not leave Janie and Tea Cake together on the muck, and any evaluation must take account of the hurricane, Tea Cake's madness, and his death by Janie's hand. Hurston has left many wondering why this marriage must end in such a violent way, and here again conventional assumptions have caused confusion. Following her interpretation of the book as literary romance, Janice Daniel sees the hurricane as the "requisite 'dragon' of [Janie's] romance quest" (72). Lupton cites this final action sequence as part of her reading of the novel in terms of evolutionary theory; under stress from the natural world, a woman has been selected as the fittest over a man (53–54). Carla Kaplan asserts that Tea Cake's death is required by the narrative logic of the novel, liberating Janie "to continue her quest and, ultimately, to satisfy her 'oldest human longing—self-revelation' with someone who *can* listen [Pheoby]" (132). Here again, Hurston comes under fire from skeptics. Ramsey, who describes Janie's life on the muck as "implausibly Edenesque" (46), calls the hurricane

73

"melodramatically gratuitous," Tea Cake's infection by rabies "fictionally arbitrary" (43), and concludes finally that Tea Cake's death is yet another mark of weakness, a way to duck several important questions: "Would Janie remain happy if tied to the seasonal cycles of grinding migrant work? Would she have money of her own that she could expect not to be taken? The novel ends conveniently before such issues arise to require resolution" (45). Even Urgo calls the novel's final sequence "wildly audacious" (53), fashioning a compliment out of the same material of Ramsey's accusation.

Recently, some have been content to label the hurricane mere plot device, and a derivative one at that, which serves solely to rid Janie of Tea Cake (or, according to Ramsey, to enact Hurston's revenge fantasy against the man she loved [46]) and titillate the reader (Lillios 91–92), but which is in any case insufficiently integrated with the novel's thematic concerns. Assuredly, the hurricane does function in these ways, but it is also more relevant to Hurston's themes than many have been willing to admit. It fits a pattern of incidents in which characters are powerless to overcome external obstacles by main force; survival depends on a careful understanding of the variables which can be controlled and those which cannot. A failed assessment leaves characters wholly at the mercy of fortune, as Motor Boat and Dick Sterrett are at the mercy of the hurricane. Other incidents fitting this pattern include Nanny's slavery experiences, Starks's bout with Death, Tea Cake's rabies, and Janie's trial. In some instances (as with Nanny and Motor Boat), fortune works in the character's favor; in others (as with Starks, Tea Cake, and Sterrett), fortune works against him, regardless of the dictates of cosmic justice. Janie's quest, if we accept that she is too weak to reverse single-handedly the sex role she is expected to play, also fits this pattern, a connection strengthened by her objective both in the quest and in escaping the hurricane waters. In both instances, Janie wishes to reach the high ground.

And here again, as with the technique of third-person narration, we must ask ourselves what the hurricane's aftermath allows Hurston to do that she otherwise could not. First, it allows her to dramatize in extreme fashion Janie's continued use of submission to control Tea Cake. During his bout with rabies, Janie never fails to answer Tea Cake's increasingly wild accusations and assertions of masculine privilege with pacifying submission: "All right, Tea Cake, jus' as you say" (172). Until the disease consumes him, her abject obedience still makes Tea Cake cry and feel ashamed of himself (171). Janie continues with her strategy of pacification to the verge of oblivion, but here Hurston is able to draw the line where submission must end; only after Tea Cake's pistol has twice clicked on an empty chamber does Janie, for the first time in their relationship, dare to command him: "Tea Cake, put down dat gun and go back tuh bed!" (175). Once Janie sees that her submission no longer functions to make her husband as she wishes him to be, she abandons the strategy entirely, shooting him with the rifle rather than follow him into death. But Janie's role-playing continues to serve her purposes, as it allows the judge in her trial to portray her as "a devoted wife trapped by unfortunate circumstances who really in firing a rifle bullet into the heart of her late husband did a great act of mercy" (179).

These events also allow Hurston to portray Janie without Tea Cake, and to re-emphasize that her happiness depends not on Tea Cake as he is, but on the Tea Cake of her dreams. As the novel comes to an end, and as Janie reflects on the sadness of what she has gone through, suddenly a vision of Tea Cake appears:

> Then Tea Cake came prancing around her where she was . . . Tea Cake, with the sun for a shawl. Of course he wasn't dead. He could never be dead until she herself had finished feeling and thinking. The kiss of his memory made pictures of love and light against the wall. Here was peace. (183–184)

The man Janie met in the store is dead, but the man whom she herself has fashioned out of his raw material still lives. Here Hurston brings the exposition of her novel full-circle; Janie is one of the women who "forget all those things they don't want to remember, and remember everything they don't want to forget. The dream is the truth" (1). This ability to fashion truth out of dreams regardless of temporal reality is what gives women like Janie their power; they are not like the pitiable men whose dreams are "mocked to death by Time" (1). Nanny, who envisions a ruling chair for Janie, has sought a future for her granddaughter where the substance of life accords with her dream of it. But, just as the ruling chair has been by custom reserved for men, so this insistence on the correspondence of dream and reality puts Janie's happiness in the hands of fortune, which Hurston notes is the predicament of the male "Watcher" of the horizon (1). Only when Janie gives up this insistence, only when she removes the fighting spirit from her soul to focus on achieving her dream through submission, is she able to become self-reliant; the reality of Tea Cake's domination of her becomes irrelevant, and so, finally, does his physical death, for despite these inconsistencies, Janie is able to make her husband into a dream-figure to serve her own needs.

Conclusion

I may here seem to portray a coldly calculating Janie, and to diminish the love she and Tea Cake share. Anyone who has read the book might protest, and rightly so, that there is no evidence for this characterization of Janie, no evidence that her love for Tea Cake and his love for her are anything but genuine. I agree with Alice Walker when she claims *Their Eyes Were Watching God* constitutes "one of the sexiest, most 'healthily' rendered heterosexual love stories in our literature" ("Zora" 17). I have not set out to challenge this claim; rather, the questions before me have been why this final marriage allows the survival of love, and why the first two do not. That traditionally-conceived sex roles are love-defeating in Janie's first two marriages is obvious; why they are not love-defeating in her third is questionable, as I have suggested. Perhaps, in answering Richard Wright's early criticisms of the book, we have been too tempted to discover the social protest he missed; Janie must therefore be the questing feminist who finds her own voice and autonomy in a marriage to a man who will allow her to actualize herself.

Evidence from the text, however, suggests that Tea Cake is no such man. Further, it is unreasonable to expect him to be: he is a southern, working-class, uneducated wanderer much more likely to be within the traditional ideology of marriage prevalent in rural, early twentieth-century America. One must assume that he is not conversant with more enlightened ideas of marriage, which were necessarily unavailable to illiterate men, not to mention undesirable to them, until much later in the century. Janie, who is incapable of single-handedly unmaking conventional marriage, must find a way to appropriate it in order to achieve her own ends. She is not responsible for externally-imposed sex roles, nor should we interpret her submission to them as whole-hearted consent to their justice; however, she has learned in her first marriages that defiance, though just, though heroic, is quixotic if not wholly disastrous. Janie's purposes, which I would suggest tend much more toward love than toward autonomy anyway, are served only when she appeals to the force of contract within conventional marriage. She achieves both self-reliance and love in spite of, not through, her third husband.

Once we adjust certain of our long-held assumptions to account for evidence they cannot explain, we are left with a well-wrought text capable of sustaining close reading. We do not have to gloss over "inconsistency" or "ambivalence" to see Janie for the heroine she is, nor do we have to resort to strained explanations that flatter our own sensibilities. This novel is clearly not the straightforward critique of gender and power in marriage that some critics claim it is, but neither is it the flawed, unfinished work of an exhausted and emotionally conflicted Zora Neale Hurston, as Ramsey claims. If we let go of our assumptions of Tea Cake as liberator, of Killicks and Starks as villains, of Janie as the unchanging feminist hero, this text is capable of answering consistently each of our questions and concerns about it. Further, we are left with a reading capable of satisfying the advocates and gate-keepers alike. Janie does not have to remain unchanged and defiant for us to recognize her covert feminism, just as other apparently subservient characters throughout the African-

American tradition do not have to defy their white masters for us to recognize their achievement of power despite an imposed racial hierarchy. Neither must we elect this book to the canon with a wink and a nudge, for charges of textual weakness, as I hope I have shown, are due to our own mistaken assumptions and not to Hurston's shoddy craftsmanship. Though one must agree with Urgo that "there is no longer any need to argue the importance of *Their Eyes Were Watching God* to American literature" (41–42), it would be best to stop coddling it. The best argument for this change in attitude is the text itself, for Hurston here demonstrates that her book has need of no one's patronage.

KERRY EMANUEL ON THE HURRICANE

Residents of the towns on the south shore of Lake Okeechobee had heard radio reports of a severe hurricane in the Caribbean and the Bahamas, but most were assured by the forecasts that it would miss Florida. The lake was already high, owing to unusually heavy rains over the previous two months and to appeals by fishermen and residents along the drainage canals to keep water levels up. Now, driven by an increasing northerly wind, the water levels on the south shore began to rise even higher. By the time the eye passed directly over the lake late on the evening of September 16, the earthen dikes had given way, and a wall of water swept inland, driven by 55 m/s (120 mph) winds. The primitive houses, many of which had been erected in the last two or three years, were instantly crushed, and the debris formed a rolling wall whose advance destroyed everything in its path. Those who escaped this onslaught sought refuge in trees, where many were killed by poisonous water moccasins also fleeing the rising water. Several people were swept miles into the Everglades; a few managed to find their way back to civilization, but many never made it. Virtually everyone who had elected to ride out the storm on the lake islands perished, as did a group of migrant workers who, ignoring warnings that strong winds would return, ventured out during the lull accompanying the passage of the eye. Some 274 women and children survived aboard two barges that miraculously rode out the storm. Others managed to clamber to the roof of a Belle Glade hotel, the only building in that town to come through relatively intact.

News of the disaster at Okeechobee was slow to reach the outside world. The nearest substantial city was West Palm Beach, some 45 miles to the east; it was itself reeling from the storm, and all telegraph lines were down. A full day and a half later, on Tuesday the eighteenth, headlines around the United States screamed news of a disaster on Florida's east coast, unaware of the far greater tragedy inland. When refugees began to trickle into West Palm Beach, the extent of the disaster slowly dawned.

To this day, the number of people who lost their lives on the shores of Okeechobee is known only very roughly. Migrant workers were not included in censuses, and at the time, state politics were dominated by northern Floridians, many of whom took a dim view of immigrants in the south. In the words of Florida's attorney general, Fred Davis, "It is mighty hard to get people in other parts of the State interested in whether they [the workers of south central Florida] perish or not." This callousness toward the welfare of the migrant workers, most of whom were black, contributed to the lack of an accurate death toll. The Red Cross initially estimated that 2,300 had died in the storm, but owing to intense pressure from officials who feared that such a large number would scare away tourists and investors, this figure was revised downward to the absurdly precise figure of 1,836, a number still repeated in contemporary literature. A simple count of the number of people reported to have been buried after the storm exceeds 2,400.[11] There can be little doubt that this was the second-worse hurricane disaster is U.S. history, exceeded only by the Galveston storm of 1900, and the second- or third-worst natural disaster, comparable to the Johnstown Flood of 1889, which killed more that 2,200. For many years afterwards, farmers cultivating land south of the lake would come across human skeletons, the last vestiges of that terrible storm.

Nine years later, in 1937, the horrors of the Okeechobee hurricane as experienced by migrant workers and their families were recounted by Zora Neale Hurston in her novel *Their Eyes Were Watching God*:

> So she was home by herself one afternoon when she saw a band of Seminoles passing by. The men walking in front and the laden, stolid women following them like burros. She had seen Indians several times in the 'Glades, in twos and threes, but this was a large party. They were headed towards the Palm Beach road and kept moving steadily. About an hour later another party appeared and went the same way. Then another just before sundown. This time she asked where they were all going and at last one of the men answered her.
> "Going to high ground. Saw-grass bloom. Hurricane coming."

Note
11. Reported in the excellent book *Killer 'Cane* by Robert Mykle.

DoVEANNA S. FULTON ON THE LEGACY OF SLAVERY

To begin this discussion of the legacy of slavery and African American heterosexual love, I start with Frederick Douglass's concept of the circle of slavery to understand how subjective points of location influence praxis of this legacy in African American lives. In his 1845 *Narrative*, Douglass describes the intensity and significance of slave songs and states,

> I did not, when a slave, understand the deep meaning of those rude and apparently incoherent songs. I was myself within the circle, so that I neither saw nor heard as those without might see and hear. They told a tale of woe which was then altogether beyond my feeble comprehension; they were tones loud, long, and deep; they breathed

the prayer and complaint of souls boiling over with the bitterest anguish. (57–58)

He goes on to admonish anyone who believes slaves sing because they are happy and points out that singing relieves sorrow and pain. Given this description, an individual's locus of knowledge determines understanding of slave expressions, particularly the oral traditions. Douglass suggests that slaves, themselves, being within the circle of slavery—or more importantly outside the realm of freedom—cannot fully comprehend the utter degradation their expressions convey because they have never experienced the breadth of freedom. For freeborn descendants of slaves this locus of knowledge is much more complicated than merely being within or without the circle of slavery. It is this complicated position that the protagonists of Zora Neale Hurston's novel *Their Eyes Were Watching God* ... occupy. With these characters, Hurston ... explore[s] the location and dislocation of love within the legacy of slavery through the main characters' dislocation vis-à-vis the circle of slavery.

Hurston ... use[s] history, particularly oral history, to reveal truths or resolutions applicable to the present dilemmas of [her] characters. Specifically, I want to focus on the ways in which [she] present[s] characters that negotiate received oral histories that are both counterhegemonic and problematic ... in order to facilitate an understanding and healing of the ruptures in male/female love relationships caused by the legacy of slavery. This legacy includes, but is not limited to, the impact of patriarchal gender ideology, domestic abuse, and the truncation of Black female sexuality. . . .

The protagonist of *Their Eyes*, Janie Crawford, confronts the history imparted orally by her grandmother, Nanny. Janie then develops a past that is both satisfying to her and usable for others. Although the oral history is passed down from Nanny who had been caught within the circle of slavery, Janie is outside the circle and, therefore, must locate her (post-Emancipation) subjective experience from this point of dislocation. Janie must contend with the culturally inscribed representations of women from African American culture that are influenced by the dominant white culture. She then rejects these representations, discovers a self in opposition to the cultural prescriptions, and proceeds on a quest of self-fulfillment. . . .

Early in the novel, Janie learns Nanny's definition of the signifier "wife" when Nanny arranges for Janie to marry Logan Killicks to ensure Janie's economic security. With the declaration, "De nigger woman is de mule uh de world" (14), Nanny voices the history of oppression of many African American women. As a slave, Nanny experienced sexual exploitation by her master and physical abuse by her jealous mistress. She was forced to run away with her newborn daughter, Leafy, and hide in the swamp until emancipation. While she never married because of her concern for Leafy's well-being, Nanny worked hard to provide a home and education for Leafy. Janie's birth is the result of Leafy's rape by a schoolteacher. After Leafy abandons her child, Nanny invests in Janie all of the hopes and desires she held for Leafy. In her concern for Janie's welfare, Nanny states, "Ah can't die easy thinkin' maybe de menfolks white or black is makin' a spit cup outa you" (19). Nanny places all of her unrealized dreams in Janie and views a life without toil as the goal to which Janie should aspire.

While Nanny's aspirations for Janie are counterhegemonic in that she does not want Janie to occupy the subservient position the dominant racist society assigns to Black women as the "mule[s] uh de world," for Janie, Nanny's wishes are problematic because they rest on material circumstances and the "economics of slavery" rather than the love and affection Janie expects in a marriage. Janie knows that she requires more than property and economic gratification to substantiate her life.

Moreover, Nanny's history does not have a space in which African American men and women exist in compatibility. Both she and her daughter were raped by white men and, according to her, Black men exploit Black women just as shamefully as white men. When Janie complains to Nanny that she has no affection for Killicks, Nanny advises her to allow time to change her mind (23). However, in order for Janie to develop a fulfilling, loving relationship with a man, she must forge an area in her life that mediates the history received from Nanny and her desire for "things sweet [with her] marriage" (23). The narrator's statement, "Finally, out of Nanny's talk and her own conjectures she made a sort of comfort for herself," illustrates Janie's initial acceptance of Nanny's narrative mediated by her own desires through which she develops a temporary consoling vision of marriage (20).

Unfortunately, Nanny's lessons are born of pragmatism based on lived experience circumscribed by the institution of slavery that does not include a mutually satisfying heterosexual relationship. With this absence, Janie's contentment with her marriage is short-lived. Hurston writes, "She knew now that marriage did not make love. Janie's first dream was dead so she became a woman" (23–24). This statement is significant given the narrator's description of female psychology in the beginning of the text: "Now women forget all those things they don't want to remember, and remember everything they don't want to forget. The dream is the truth" (1). If Janie only becomes a woman after she finds emptiness in marriage, then her selective memory is at work because she "forget[s]" the painful history Nanny shares and remembers only the ecstasy of her gilded fantasy.

Through her experience, Janie learns that—although exploration of life's possibilities is essential to self-fulfillment—selective amnesia is detrimental to independence and subjectivity. When Janie meets Joe Starks, she sees the possibilities life with him may offer. However, before she embarks on a new life, "Janie pulled back a long time because [Joe] did not represent sun-up and pollen and blooming trees, but he spoke for far horizons. He spoke of change and chance. Still she hung back. The memory of Nanny was still powerful and strong" (28). This passage demonstrates the conscious decision Janie makes to break out of the confining subject position of "wife" defined by Nanny and Killicks and to desert the oral history she's been taught. That Janie recognizes the "far horizons" and "change and chance" Joe represents suggests her rejection of the oral history Nanny presents. Although she feels the weight of this history and cannot easily disregard it, nevertheless, she can conceive of a different way of existing than that dictated by her community.

However, that Janie disregards the fact that Joe "did not represent sun-up and pollen and blooming trees" shows the consequences of compromising the self. For when Janie chooses to leave Killicks for Joe, she experiences patriarchal domination by Joe and constrictions and pressures imposed through the cultural representations surrounding her position as the "mayor's wife." . . .

Although Nanny's aspirations for Janie are constructed on an aspect of bourgeois philosophy that emphasizes privilege and wealth, her experiences during and after slavery indicate the sense of strength and integrity African American women must hold for themselves to withstand oppressive circumstances. Nanny's flight from an impending whipping because of the mistress' jealousy, her choice to remain a single mother to ensure Leafy would not experience abuse at the hands of a stepfather, and the purchase of a home so that Janie would know stability and security demonstrate Nanny's refusal to compromise herself and her position as a mother/grandmother. Nanny declares, "Ah wanted to preach a great sermon about colored women sittin' on high, but they wasn't no pulpit for me" (15). That Nanny desires to tell a narrative of instruction about Black women's triumphs is a testament to the instruction inherent in her own oral history. Yet because her society does not contain a space for her to speak to a public audience, she resolves to relate her personal narrative to Janie, an audience of one. Understood in this way this resolution exemplifies Black feminist orality. In opposition to the restrictions placed on her, Nanny manages to leave her narrative with Janie (both in her head and on her person). The narrative is meant to empower Janie so that she will not suffer as Nanny did. Unfortunately, Janie ignores Nanny's history and, thereby, subjects herself to Joe's domination. It is not until after Joe's death and her relationship with Tea Cake that Janie's experiences can compare to Nanny's and she is able to understand and define herself in opposition to the community's expectations and live her life in the manner that most pleases her.

Janie views the love she and Tea Cake share and the work they do as her life's fulfillment. The mutual labor between Janie and Tea Cake is a manifestation of her negotiation of Nanny's history to create a functional relationship in her own present. Although Nanny would have Janie liberated from work with "uh prop tuh lean on all [her] bawn days" (22), the satisfaction found in their joint industry is more fulfilling than what Janie experienced in either one of her previous marriages. In response to Tea Cake's worry that her working demonstrated his inability to provide for her, Janie contends, "It's mo' nicer than settin' round dese quarters all day. Clerkin' in dat store wuz hard, but heah, we ain't got nothin' tuh do but do our work and come home and love" (127). Tea Cake's concern is representative of the economic constraints that impede the progress of many Black heterosexual relationships. . . . [W]ith Tea Cake, Janie experiences self-fulfillment by doing all the things and going to all the places she desires. She declares, "Ah done been tuh de horizon and back and now Ah kin set mah house and live by comparisons" (182). Janie explores life's possibilities and measures her fulfillment and subjectivity to those around her.

As opposed to Nanny's view that "Dat's de very prong all us black women gits hung on. Dis love" (22), Janie is not paralyzed by love. Tea Cake and Janie's love is not static but dynamic and unique. In response to the townspeople's reaction to her relationship with Tea Cake, Janie remarks, "Love is lak de sea. It's uh movin' thing, but still and all, it takes its shape from de shore it meets, and it's different with every shore" (182). Janie reconfigures the concepts of love she has encountered from Nanny and her community and experiences a powerful relationship in which she becomes self-defined and fulfilled.

This self-definition is manifested through her refusal to conform to community standards of race, class, and gender. Kubitschek identifies Janie and Tea Cake's love relationship as a form of the African American oral tradition of call and response in which Tea Cake and Janie alternate in their roles of performer and audience (64). This role switching corresponds to their negotiation of traditional gender roles. While Janie works in the fields with Tea Cake, he helps her prepare meals. Similarly, the dynamic nature of love Janie describes parallels her negotiation of history and tradition. She shapes subject positions such as woman, wife, and lover into a form that best defines her.

Despite the love Janie finds, she must still recognize and face the legacy of slavery that informs her life. Both the segregated Jim Crow society she and Tea Cake reenter in Palm Beach and the reaction of Tea Cake's friends following her acquittal for his death represent the inescapable limits placed on African Americans in a racial society. Similarly, Janie's experience of domestic abuse by Tea Cake because of the perceived threat to their relationship by Mrs. Turner's brother is a reflection of slavery's legacy in African American life. Although Mrs. Turner's brother is Black, Mrs. Turner's adoration of white features and description of her brother as having "dead straight hair" (136) serve to represent him as a "white" rival to Tea Cake. This representation recalls white male sexual exploitation of Black females and Black male powerlessness against this exploitation during slavery. Thus, Tea Cake's rage, though misdirected, is a reaction to this powerlessness. This misguided rage, coupled with patriarchy, produces domestic violence.

The violence Janie experiences results, in part, from the residuum of the patriarchal slave institution. The sense of ownership and domination of another human to the point of physical abuse are aspects of slavery that sustain Black domestic violence. These aspects surface within marriage and mirror the power relations inherent in slavery. Alice Walker speaks to this phenomenon and contends,

At the root of the denial of easily observable and heavily documented sexist brutality in the Black community . . . is our deep, painful refusal to accept the fact that we are not only descendants of slaves, but we are also descendants of slave owners. And that just as we have had to struggle to rid ourselves of slavish behaviors we must as ruthlessly eradicate any desire to be mistress or "master."[4]

Note
4. As quoted in Patricia Hill Collins's *Black Feminist Thought* (186).

STEPHEN SPENCER ON HURSTON'S CONTRIBUTION TO THE CANON

Although critics in the 1950s, 1960s, and 1970s commented occasionally on Hurston's work, especially *Their Eyes Were Watching God*, not until feminist and cultural criticism emerged as important interpretive strategies in the academy, did a space exist for the study of Hurston's work. Like feminist critics and writers, scholars established black studies programs in colleges and universities. Just as feminism in the 1960s and 1970s gained ground in the worlds of academe and literary criticism, so black critics and writers worked to change the canon in other ways. The critics Houston A. Baker, Jr., Henry Louis Gates, Jr., and Addison Gayle, Jr., would articulate a new Black Aesthetic that placed the sources of contemporary black literature and culture in the communal music and oral folk tradition. Baker's *Blues, Ideology, and Afro-American Literature: A Vernacular Theory*, for example, explored the ways tales, songs, oratory, sermons, blues, and jazz made black culture in America distinctive. Thus, texts like Zora Neale Hurston's *Mules and Men* exploring the folk culture of rural Florida would become important. At the same time the critics Barbara Christian, Gloria Hull, Barbara Smith, and Mary Helen Washington and the writers Toni Cade Bambara, Audre Lorde, and Alice Walker would shape a distinctive black feminism, making a place for writers like Zora Neale Hurston, whose rediscovery was initiated by Alice Walker. The efforts to establish such programs paved the way for similar ethnic studies programs and the revision of the canon.

Now that *Their Eyes Were Watching God* has assured Hurston's status in the canon, how can scholars interrogate the novel in the context of the canonicity it has achieved? What does its canonicity reveal about current assumptions about multiethnic literature in general and race, gender, and power in particular? What does the status of *Their Eyes Were Watching God* reveal about the directions that discussions of canonicity and multiethnic literature are taking?

The canonical success of *Their Eyes Were Watching God* suggests that Hurston's work anticipated the direction canonicity and multiethnic literature have taken. Hurston's work moved beyond prevailing theories of identity construction in the twentieth century into what Mikhail Bakhtin and Robert Young call "hybridity," what postcolonial theorist Homi Bhabha calls "the third space," what gender studies calls "the space-in-between," and what Chicano/a scholars and writers Virgilio Elizondo and Gloria Anzaldúa call "mestizo/a" and "borderlands." Such attempts to mix, blur, and cross are certainly not a recent phenomenon. In his thorough history and analysis of the origin and development of the concept of hybridity, Robert Young argues that many English writers of the present and past have written "almost obsessively about the uncertain crossing and invasion of identities," whether of class, gender, culture, or race, to such an extent that we might say such crossing is "the dominant *motif* of much English fiction" (2–3). This obsession, Young claims, has always existed because attempts to identify the essentialness of Englishness have never been successful. Young's analysis applies equally to definitions of Americanness, which were rooted in Anglophile conceptions of identity as the idea of America as a nation formed. Attempts to essentialize an American identity have never been successful, because it was never really possible. Ethnically mixed writers and writers excluded from the mainstream definitions of Americanness have always known this.

Some critics argue that attempts at hybridity, border crossing, and cultural relativism inevitably run the risk of reinforcing the very lines they seek to blur or redefine. Gerry Smyth argues that "hybridity is hegemonically recuperable, easily absorbed by those with an interest in denying the validity of a coherent discourse of resistance" (43). Smyth argues that hybridity, despite its claims for resistance and redefinition of border, could instead reinforce the stereotypical assumptions which created the very borders it seeks to blur. The danger, for Smyth, is that hybridity may be "re-absorbed into disabling neo-colonialist narratives" (52). Hybridity, for Smyth, denies the ability of the other to rationalize his or her position, and thus undermines resistance. He concludes his argument by suggesting that a politics organized around border crossing denies the most powerful form of resistance: silence. Postcolonial criticism, according to Young, has also reinforced the very categories it seeks to resist by constructing two antithetical groups, with the second group depending for its existence on the first group, which was an artificial construction in the first place. Multiculturalism, Young argues, has done the same thing by encouraging different groups to "reify their individual and different identities at their most different" (5).

Hurston does not really seem to care if her discourse will be "re-absorbed into disabling neo-colonialist narratives" or reify difference. But she certainly cares about speaking. Institutionally organized power does all it can to silence; therefore, Hurston is actively resisting. Silence could also be interpreted as concession rather than resistance. Isn't silence what the oppressor wants? It is certainly what Joe Starks demands, and it is what the white court commands at the end of *Their Eyes Were Watching God*. Janie's rendition of her own story is then a significant act of resistance *and* redefinition. It resists essentialism and dismantles race as inherent and self-evident, revealing it as a construct and means of oppression. It redefines the borders of race and gender through Janie's self-definition. Hurston replaces essentializing categories of difference with a new model that reflects the current, and I would argue the next, moment in multiethnic theory. Hurston expresses hybridity, a third space, a borderland through both sex (Janie as literal racial hybrid) and language (the blending of male/female language, standard English/dialect, formal prose/folklore). Thus, Zora Neale Hurston is a writer who reflects the current moment of literary history. Hurston, a black woman drawing consciously on a folk tradition in her work, presents a vision of American life that can be read with and against evolving notions of race, gender, and power in American culture.

META G. CARSTARPHEN ON
FANTASY AND REALITY IN THE NOVEL

Readers plunging into *Their Eyes Were Watching God* will find a coming-of-age novel like no other for many distinctive reasons. First, the story centers around Janie Mae Woods, a Southern African American woman born in poverty and raised by her maternal grandmother, called Nanny. Janie is an unwitting heroine. She has no particular distinction according to race or class. She has no grand dreams or ambitions that she expresses, other than an impatient yearning when she was 16, to see the world "be made" (p. 11). Second, all of the characters, save the most minor of ones, are African American. The 1930s society that Janie moves in, while proscribed by the racial segregation of the era, is never disempowered by that fact. Social status and power relationships, especially as they exist between men and women, define themselves on terms nearly, if not virtually, free from the dynamics of racial politics. Third, Hurston writes much of this novel using the language and dialect of the Southern folk she grew up around and whom she spent her professional career documenting. Alternating with clear passages that offer prosaic descriptions and crisp details, *Their Eyes* offers a reading experience that is both anchored in a specific place and time and anchorless in a compelling, universal story of love and choice.

Janie's adventures in love begin when an innocent kiss from a teenaged friend awakens uncertain stirrings. But to Nanny, such experimentation points to future problems. Her solution is to marry Janie off to Logan Killicks, an older neighbor who owns 60 acres and, as such, represents material stability to the aging grandmother worried about the future of her ward. Naively, Janie waits for marriage to turn into love. But when she discovers that the two can be totally separate things, she concludes that her first dream is "dead"; therefore, she has become "a woman" (Z. N. Hurston, 1937/1999, p. 25).

After a while, Janie literally runs away from this loveless marriage, captivated by the more sophisticated courtship and bold dreams of Joe Starks. With her beloved Nanny dead and a first husband expecting her to labor like a mule on their land, Janie imagines a happier future with the charismatic Starks. They marry and set off for a new town, where Starks becomes mayor and owner of the town's most important business, a general store. But as Starks fulfills his personal ambition of becoming "uh big voice" (p. 46), Janie finds her role diminished as his partner. Although she shares in the work of maintaining the store and in ceremonial duties as the Mayor's wife, she finds that her husband sees any attention shown to her as a threat to the focus upon himself. He admonishes her not to talk freely in the store and insists that she hide her long and beautiful hair under a scarf When she tries to express her fears over how success has kept them apart, Starks ignores her, insisting that her role as his wife should make her glad since it makes a "big [important] woman" out of her (p. 46).

When Starks dies after 20 years of marriage, Janie frees her hair and also her spirit to new possibilities. Nearing 40 years old, Janie has maturity, vitality, and material comfort as the widow of the richest man in town. And while eager suitors press for her attention, Janie realizes that she likes the new "freedom feeling" she is experiencing (p. 90). While she continues in this pleasure, a new one surprises her in the form of a free-spirited, younger man named Tea Cake. Unfazed by her status, Tea Cake invites her to play checkers, go fishing, and, eventually, share his life as a seasonal worker harvesting sugar cane, tomatoes, and string beans. Janie runs off and marries Tea Cake, confiding in her best friend, Pheoby, that she is determined to live her way, after a lifetime of trying to live "Grandma's way" (p. 114).

The rest of the novel takes off as Janie experiences her new life and her new love. Janie and Tea Cake laugh and argue, work and play, but their lives together seem bound by partnership and love. And, what animates Janie is the realization in her life, finally, of a successful prescription for love—one that allows her to create a "coequal relationship" through cooperation. Galician's (2004) Rx #6 for healthy coupleship, the ability to create "coequality," rests on an ability to challenge established gender roles. In *Their Eyes*, Janie and Tea Cake's relationship completely inverts the social roles that had been portrayed as models throughout and that Janie herself had experienced, in which a dependent woman was paired with an independent, "stronger" male (Myth #6; Galician, 2004). But rather than basking in the protection such a relationship was supposed to provide, Janie despaired. Instead, she thrived in a relationship with a man whom her community deemed unworthy of her because he was younger, less successful, and of a different social class.

Such inversions in Hurston's personal life never succeeded, however. Her husbands and her lover who inspired *Their Eyes* were all younger and socially less prominent than she. Yet in each case, the desire to be a couple never overcame a shared inability to unite over life goals. Just as Myth #9 warns, an unrealistic view of romantic love cannot overcome the challenges of two people living together who have "totally opposite values." For Zora, whose romantic imprint from her formative years fixed upon an unyielding dichotomy in which work opposed love, the bridge needed to span the two perhaps seemed impossible to build in her own life.

And even in her fictional world, the perfect love she created in *Their Eyes* did not end perfectly. Tea Cake dies tragically, leaving Janie a widow once more. Her grief is tempered, however, by her loving memories of a partner who would never be dead until Janie herself "had finished feeling and thinking" (p. 193).

Conclusion: Romantic Fantasy, Romantic Reality?

Since their nascent forms at the start of the 20th century, popular mass media have shaped our images of gender, sexuality, and gender roles through intentional constructions and strategies (Carstarphen & Zavoina, 1999). Hurston's autobiography *Dust Tracks on a Road* (1942/1996) attributes her powerful characters of Janie and Tea Cake to her internal need to grieve for a failed romance. Yet, the ambitious, socially aware, and independent-minded woman that she was also seemed to have known the external need for a heroine like no other. Since its revival in the 1980s, *Their Eyes* has stayed continuously in print as a novel and was transformed into a made-for-television movie featuring megastar Halle Berry as Janie and co-produced by media icons Oprah Winfrey and Quincy Jones. New audiences can now debate Janie's choices and evaluate the story's authenticity as a romance. For her part, author Zora Neale Hurston made painful choices in the pursuit of perfected romance in her own life. In the end, she gave herself and others the solace of a dream made into literature, becoming a timeless prescription for love.

Works by Zora Neale Hurston

Jonah's Gourd Vine. 1934.

Mules and Men. 1935.

Their Eyes Were Watching God. 1937.

Tell My Horse. 1938.

Moses, Man of the Mountain. 1939.

Dust Tracks on a Road. 1942.

Seraph on the Suwanee. 1949.

I Love Myself When I Am Laughing . . . & Then Again When I Am Looking Mean and Impressive: A Zora Neale Hurston Reader. Ed. Alice Walker. 1979.

The Sanctified Church. Ed. Toni Cade Bambara. 1981.

Spunk: The Selected Short Stories of Zora Neale Hurston. 1985.

Annotated Bibliography

Awkward, Michael, ed. *New Essays on Their Eyes Were Watching God*. Cambridge: Cambridge University Press, 1990.

Michael Awkward's introduction discusses Hurston's own awareness of the cultural forces that would likely result in an undervaluing of her work. He offers a close look at what some of these forces were and what the effects of multiculturalism have had on the novel's restoration. The "new" essays in this volume, written by critics who have previously written on Hurston, specifically address some of the issues involved in re-establishing Hurston as an important American writer. This volume is an excellent resource for serious students beginning a study of Hurston's work.

Bona, Mary Jo and Irma Maini, eds. *Multiethnic Literature and Canon Debates*. Albany: State University of New York Press, 2006.

This collection of essays takes on the controversial issue of the place of multiethnic literature in the American canon. The editors reflect on specific titles (*Their Eyes Were Watching God* is one) and discuss the standards, values, and assumptions that are used to either establish or challenge a work of literature. For students caught up in these impassioned controversies, this volume is essential reading.

Cronin, Gloria L., ed. *Critical Essays on Zora Neale Hurston*. New York: G. K. Hall, 1998.

Beginning with Hurston's first novel, *Jonah's Gourd Vine* (1934), the collected essays in the volume cover all of her published work, including her autobiography, *Dust Tracks on a Road* (1942), her folklore writings, and her short stories (*The Complete Stories* (1995). In her introduction, Cronin discusses the critical reception each work received.

Emanuel, Kelly. *Divine Wind: The History and Science of Hurricanes*. Oxford: Oxford University Press, 2005.

This one-of-a-kind book combines paintings, poems, graphs, historical accounts, and aerial and ground photography with discussion of advancing scientific knowledge to give a comprehensive picture of hurricanes and their diverse effects on land and populations throughout history. It is particularly interesting to read about the San Felipe hurricane that struck the Lake Okeechobee region of Florida that was indirectly responsible for the end of the Janie-Tea Cake love affair and Tea Cake's death, but the whole book is fascinating for anyone interested in wild weather events.

Fulton, DoVeanna S. *Speaking Power: Black Feminist Orality in Women's Narratives of Slavery*. Albany: State University of New York Press, 2006.

In her prefatory remarks, the author relates incidents from her personal history that subtly conveyed to others perceptions of her as a "second class citizen" and contrasting incidents that emboldened her to resist the invidious effects of racism. In her discussion of *Their Eyes Were Watching God*, Fulton uses Janie Crawford's struggles and triumphs and passages from old slave narratives to illustrate the liberating potential of "testimony" and other features of black oral tradition. The author assumes her readers will have some familiarity with the subject matter.

Galician, Mary-Lou and Debra L. Merskin, eds. *Critical Thinking About Sex, Love, and Romance in the Mass Media*. Mahwah, N.J.: Lawrence Erlbaum Associates, Publishers, 2007.

As the title promises, this substantial volume (408 pages) offers a collection of essays examining the media presentation of sex and love (myths, fantasies, and realities) in romantic relationships. *Their Eyes Were Watching God* is discussed in this context. The editors have drawn from all the contemporary media sources—television, magazines, the Internet, movies, pop music, and books—to illustrate a general failure by the mass media to provide healthy and mature portrayals of romantic love relationships. Popular favorites—*Sex and the City, The Sopranos,*

The Wedding Planner, You've Got Mail—are among the mass media productions discussed.

Goldstein, Philip. *Communities of Cultural Value: Reception Study, Political Differences, and Literary History*. Lanham, Md.: Lexington Books, 2001.

This examination of literary theory is most suitable for students advanced in the study of English and American literature. For the general reader it provides some interesting insights about the different ways works of literature have been received by the literary communities they have been intended for. Goldstein is also interested in why certain works go in and out of favor. In the case of *Their Eyes Were Watching God*, he discusses the novel's early mixed reception followed by an almost complete disappearance from public view until the late 1970s and 1980s, when Alice Walker paid sufficient attention to its author to restore it to its current status.

Green, Suzanne Disheroon and Lisa Abney, eds. *Songs of the New South: Writing Contemporary Louisiana*. Westport, Conn.: Greenwood Press, 2001.

This collection of essays is organized around the multilayered aspects of Southern culture, with special focus on Louisiana. Zora Neal Hurston was attracted to the pagan subculture in New Orleans, and the essay on *Their Eyes Were Watching God* traces this influence.

Hemenway, Robert. *Zora Neale Hurston: A Literary Biography*. Urbana: University of Illinois Press, 1977.

Hemenway explains in his prefatory notes that when he became interested in writing about Hurston, there was scant information about her life to draw upon. A sign and cause of her imminent return to public view and to considerable popularity, as well, was the grant awarded in 1970–71 to the author from the National Endowment for the Humanities to begin the research necessary to bring her out of obscurity. In 1973, Alice Walker made her famous pilgrimage in search of Hurston's grave. The combined efforts of Hemenway and Walker are credited for the literary status Hurston's works currently enjoy.

Lester, Neal A. *Understanding Zora Neale Hurston's "Their Eyes Were Watching God."* Westport, Conn.: Greenwood Press, 1999.

This well-researched book is an excellent introduction to the novel for first-time readers. The novel is considered thematically and historically but is also used as a reason to look at other relevant features of African American culture. Included are photographs depicting the injustices and smoldering racism of the Jim Crow era and discussions of Ebonics and rap music. Interviews with people living during this era and in the same region as Hurston's characters expand the reader's understanding of the novel's context.

McGowan, Todd. *The Feminine "No!": Psychoanalysis and the New Canon.* Albany: State University of New York Press, 2001.

Two features of McGowan's study make it appropriate reading for advanced students. First, the author draws on Jacques Lacan's work on psychoanalytic theory, which requires substantial familiarity with Freudian theories. Second, it addresses itself to students engaged in the current debates over what standards to use in determining which works of literature rightly belong in the contemporary canon. It is possible, however, to read the author's approach to the four novels he considers (*Their Eyes Were Watching God* is one of four) without understanding all the references.

Miles, Diana. *Women, Violence, & Testimony in the Works of Zora Neale Hurston.* New York: Peter Lang Publishing, Inc., 2003.

This sophisticated study attempts to enlarge the parameters for understanding the work of Zora Neale Hurston. Specifically, it looks at the portrayals of violence against women—calling them "trauma testimonies"—and suggests that Hurston was both consciously and unconsciously delineating universally painful experiences, the retelling of which forms a connection among women and an occasion for healing in the wider community. This perspective invites a rereading of Hurston's works which have traditionally been read as time- and region-specific.

Wall, Cheryl A., ed. *Zora Neale Hurston's "Their Eyes Were Watching God": A Casebook*. Oxford: Oxford University Press, 2000.

This volume assembles previously published essays by well-known critics who have contributed to the relatively recent surge of appreciation for Hurston and *Their Eyes Were Watching God*. Some of these essays also suggest new directions literary criticism of the novel might take.

Contributors

Harold Bloom is Sterling Professor of the Humanities at Yale University. He is the author of 30 books, including *Shelley's Mythmaking, The Visionary Company, Blake's Apocalypse, Yeats, A Map of Misreading, Kabbalah and Criticism, Agon: Toward a Theory of Revisionism, The American Religion, The Western Canon,* and *Omens of Millennium: The Gnosis of Angels, Dreams, and Resurrection. The Anxiety of Influence* sets forth Professor Bloom's provocative theory of the literary relationships between the great writers and their predecessors. His most recent books include *Shakespeare: The Invention of the Human,* a 1998 National Book Award finalist, *How to Read and Why, Genius: A Mosaic of One Hundred Exemplary Creative Minds, Hamlet: Poem Unlimited, Where Shall Wisdom Be Found?,* and *Jesus and Yahweh: The Names Divine.* In 1999, Professor Bloom received the prestigious American Academy of Arts and Letters Gold Medal for Criticism. He has also received the International Prize of Catalonia, the Alfonso Reyes Prize of Mexico, and the Hans Christian Andersen Bicentennial Prize of Denmark.

Mary Helen Washington teaches English at the University of Maryland. She has been published in *The Massachusetts Review, Ms* Magazine, *TV Guide,* and *The Washington Post.* In 1986 she won the Zora Neale Hurston Creative Scholarship Award.

Henry Louis Gates Jr. is director of the W.E.B. Du Bois Institute for Afro American Research and the W.E.B. Du Bois Professor of the Humanities at Harvard University. His publications include *Loose Canons: Notes on the Culture Wars* (1992) and *The Signifying Monkey: Towards a Theory of Afro-American Literary Criticism* (1998). He is the general editor of the *Norton Anthology of Afro-American Literature.* Gates has been instrumental in opening up discussion of Africa with a view that challenges the "primitive," "dark continent" stereotypes. He created a series of six one-hour programs for PBS called *The Wonders of the African World.*

Neal A. Lester teaches African American literature at Arizona State University. In 1995 he published *Ntozake Shange: A Critical Study of the Plays.* He has also published work on Alice Walker.

Philip Goldstein has taught in both the English and Women's Studies programs at the University of Delaware. He is the author of *The Politics of Literary Criticism: An Introduction to Marxist Critical Theory* (1990), editor of *Styles of Cultural Activism: From Theory and Pedagogy to Women, Indians, and Communism* (1993), and co-editor of *Reception Study: Theory, Practice, History* (2000).

Ted McGowan teaches English at Southwest Texas State University.

Pamela Glenn Menke is professor of English at Regis College. Her research interest is the impact of race and gender in literature of the American South and in twentieth-century literature written by women of color.

Diana Miles teaches English at Morehouse College in Georgia. Her research interests include historical and individual trauma as relayed through literature.

Shawn E. Miller has been published in *The Southern Literary Journal* and *The Southern Quarterly.*

Kerry Emanuel teaches in the atmospheric sciences department at the Massachusetts Institute of Technology. He is among the group of scientists who first noticed an interaction between hurricanes and climate change.

DoVeanna S. Fulton teaches English at Arizona State University. Her research interests include the folk and oral traditions in African American writing.

Stephen Spencer is associate professor of English at Wilmington College of Ohio. His other published work has focused on Pearl Buck, Eric Jerome Dickey, and race issues.

Meta G. Carstarphen is an associate dean and professor at the Gaylord College of Journalism and Mass Communication at the University of Oklahoma. She has done professional work in community race relations, nonprofit public relations, and cross-cultural integrated communication. Her latest publication is a textbook titled *Writing PR: A Multimedia Approach* (2004).

Acknowledgments

Mary Helen Washington, "'I Love the Way Janie Crawford Left Her Husbands': Zora Neale Hurston's Emergent Female Hero." From *Zora Neale Hurston's "Their Eyes Were Watching God": A Casebook*, edited by Cheryl A. Wall, pp. 27–40. © 2000 by Oxford University Press, Inc.

Henry Louis Gates Jr., "Zora Neale Hurston and the Speakerly Text." From *Zora Neale Hurston's "Their Eyes Were Watching God": A Casebook*, edited by Cheryl A. Wall, pp. 59–116. © 2000 by Oxford University Press, Inc.

Neal A. Lester, "'Them Folks Ain't Talkin' Right': Glancing at the Ebonics Debate." From *Understanding Zora Neale Hurston's Their Eyes Were Watching God.* Greenwood Press, pp. 31–35. Copyright © 1999 by Neal A. Lester. Reproduced with permission of Greenwood Publishing Group, Inc., Westport, CT.

Phillip Goldstein, "The Critical Realism or Black Modernism?: The Reception of *Their Eyes Were Watching God.*" From *Communities of Cultural Value: Reception Study, Political Differences, and Literary History*, pp. 190–192, 198. © 2001 by Lexington Books.

Todd McGowan, "Liberation and Domination: Their Eyes Were Watching God and the Evolution of Capital." Reprinted by permission from *The Feminine "No!": Psychoanalysis and the New Canon*, State University of New York Press, pp. 85–100. © 2001 State University of New York. All rights reserved.

Pamela Glenn Menke, "'Black cat bone and snake wisdom': Orleanian Hoodoo, Haitian Voodoo, and Rereading *Their Eyes Were Watching God.*" From *Songs of the New South:*

Index

Self, 39–40, 42
Self-doubt, 58
Self-reflective voice, 41
Seraph on the Suwanee (Hurston), 13
Silence, 35–36, 89
Slave songs, 80–81
Slavery, legacy of, 80–87
Smyth, Gerry, 88–89
Speakerly text, 38
Spencer, Stephen, 87–90
Sun, 10

T

Tea Cake (*Their Eyes Were Watching God*), 10–11, 17, 18
  death of, 31, 51, 72, 73–74, 76
  domination by, 51, 56–59
  relationship between Janie and, 15, 25–31, 51, 55–59, 66, 68–70, 74–77, 85–86, 91–92
  voice of, 35
Tell My Horse (Hurston), 12, 63
Testimonies, 68
Their Eyes Were Watching God (Hurston). *See also specific characters*
  authorial intrusion into, 29
  autobiographical elements in, 62, 68–70, 72
  as bildungsroman, 21, 90
  characters in, 18–19
  conclusion of, 10–11, 73–78
  conflicted readings of, 73–78
  context of, 14–17
  female characters in, 7–8
  female identity in, 66–72
  feminist critique of, 33–37
  narrative structure of, 42–43, 71, 74–75

place of, in canon, 17, 87–90
plot summary of, 20–31
Pride and Prejudice compared with, 47–50
publication of, 13
reviews of, 15–16
voodoo elements in, 61–66
Third-person narration, 74–75
Thornton, Jerome, 55–56

U

Urgo, Joseph, 51, 59n13

V

Violence, 57, 69–71, 86
Voice, 38–39
  female, 20, 33–37
  male, 36
  narrative, 20, 42
  oral, 38
  self-reflective, 41
Voodoo, 61–66

W

Walker, Alice, 16–17, 76, 86–87
Washington, Mary Helen, 33–37
Whitman, Walt, 11
Willis, Susan, 62
Women
  as objects, 33–34
  repression in, 7–8
  silencing of, 35–36
Wright, Richard, 15, 17, 37–43

Y

Young, Robert, 88

Z

Zora Neale Hurston (Hemenway), 17